SEE YOU AROUND
A PANTOMIME OF BYGONE FUN AND FROLIC

A retired SailorBoy, home from the sea, looked at an old postcard and dreamed about it. Suddenly the old postcard came alive. Once again he revisited the seaside resort where he had enjoyed fun with friends as a younger man. Out of the card stepped a young lady, a dancer, who began to show the SailorBoy around the Magic Mile - a place in the other world where all the funny postcard people had gone and where they still lived and sang their oldtime songs.

In this time-warp, such characters came alive as the Grand Dame Knowitall; Lotsadebt, the villain and his pal BillBailiff; Skinny, the walking bones; Snooty, the upper-class drunk; a few seaside blondes; the Bearded Woman and the Fat Lady. Outstanding among the dancers was the young lady from the Good Old Days.

LIFE OF DREW CARSON

Sam Drew Carson was born in the North of Ireland and educated there at Wellington College and the Ulster Polytechnic. He completed his education in the USA at New Mexico Highlands University and the University of Arkansas and has traveled widely in North America, around the Atlantic and in Europe.

Drew worked as a seaman and fish-gutter in Vestmannaeyjar off the coast of Iceland. He lived and worked in the Irish and Western Isles Gaeltachts and was married in Welsh-speaking Carmarthen after which he honeymooned in Belfast. He has told his stories, composed and sung his songs, seeking storylines in Bristol and the English Westcountry. Drew has also lived and written in Nashville, Tennessee, in the wooded hills of Mid-America and from the Appalachians to the Ozarks. This was the culture that gave rise to the now worldwide Scotch-Irish country music.

In the USA, he also worked beside the bayous of the French-speaking Cajuns in the South and among the Western Spanish-speaking Navajos, Apaches and Pueblos of the Sangre de Cristo Mountains in New Mexico.

Drew has sailed far into the seas of old Gaelic and Oriental legend. After many years searching for inspiration for story and music, the author is still traveling and writing.

BOOKS BY THE SAME AUTHOR

ZENISUB
Fun and Games in Businezz
ISBN: 978-0-9561435-2-5

GOOD FOR A LAUGH
Six Funny Playscripts for Amateurs
ISBN: 978-0-9561435-3-2

HOME WITH A GOOD COMPANION
Amateur Pantomime Scripts for a Merry Winter
ISBN: 978-0-9561435-4-9

CLASSIC EUROPEAN LYRICS
Translated from the Gaelic, the French and Spanish
ISBN: 978-0-9561435-6-3

COMMONWEALTH
An Introduction to Business Economics
ISBN: 978-0-9561435-7-0

MISSING PERSONS
Detective Felix O'Neill in a Crime Adventure
ISBN: 978-0-9561435-8-7

WEREWOLF MURDERS
Detective Felix O'Neill in a Crime Adventure
ISBN: 978-0-9561435-9-4

ORIENTAL GOVERNESS
Detective Felix O'Neill in a Crime Adventure
ISBN: 978-1-908184-00-9

EASTER AND THE SPRINGTIME
Five Amateur Playscripts about New Life
ISBN: 978-1-908184-02-3

WALLWAVE THE YOUNG SEA WARRIOR
Adventures of War Queens and Battle Heroes
ISBN: 978-1-908184-03-0

WALLWAVE THE SEA PRINCE
Adventures of War Queens and Battle Heroes
ISBN: 978-1-908184-04-7

WALLWAVE THE SEA KING
Adventures of War Queens and Battle Heroes
ISBN: 978-1-908184-05-4

THAT SILVER SHORE
Easter Musical with Ten Songs
ISBN: 978-1-908184-06-1

THE OTHER SIDE
Halloween Masque of Demons and Delusions
ISBN: 978-1-908184-07-8

SEE YOU AROUND
Pantomime of Bygone Fun and Frolic
ISBN: 978-1-908184-08-5

SEE YOU AROUND
A Pantomime of Bygone
Fun and Frolic

DREW CARSON

order from: https://www.createspace.com/4137031

Legals

Published by S. A. Carson,
29 Northleaze, Long Ashton, Bristol BS41 9HS, UK
Publisher's email: verygoodreading@googlemail.com

ISBN: 978-1-908184-08-5

CONTENTS

Page

ABOUT THE PLAY

A retired SailorBoy, home from the sea, looked at an old postcard and dreamed about it. Suddenly the old postcard came alive. Once again he revisited the seaside resort where he had enjoyed fun with friends as a younger man. Out of the card stepped a young lady, a dancer, who began to show the SailorBoy around the Magic Mile - a place in the other world where all the funny postcard people had gone and where they still lived and sang their oldtime songs.

In this time-warp, such characters came alive as the Grand Dame Knowitall; Lotsadebt, the dwarf and his pal Bill Bailiff; Skinny, the walking bones; Snooty, the upper-class drunk; a few seaside blondes; the Bearded Woman and the Fat Lady. Outstanding among the dancers was the young lady from the Good Old Days.

At first, the SailorBoy was inclined to reminisce about the music and about the places where the music was played but many places seemed to have changed. Still, he began to find that the old figures from the postcard were alive, hidden here and there among the crowds in Old Seaside.

Old Seaside was like a composite of many different bygone seaside resorts. One was famous for its oysters, another for its tea and another for its fish and chips. All three were still going strong in this old postcard come alive.

The long promenade was a paved walk, lined with freak shows and cafes and bars where the brass band still marched up and down, followed by young people laughing and joking and pushing each other. It was a happy scene caused by the good marching music. The SailorBoy noted that you seldom hear the good marching music today. Today's brass bands seemed to be intent on showing off their musical techniques, their ability to jump from one tempo or set of notes to another. "What a clever band we are," they seemed to be saying.

The old brass band had not been so smart, not at all but they played simple, melodious music that you could remember and sing to yourself in the bath.

The brash, naughty schoolboy humor of the old days was still here in Old Seaside. It had not yet given way to modern porn or racketeering or reckless gambling. The oldtime bingo had been more fun than figures. The prizes had been stuffed toys not fortunes and speaking of fortunes the gypsies would have told you the silliest stories for a penny.

Later, the streets had become filled with big bookie chains that always had a secret reason not to pay out anything much to anyone. Unusual betting patterns seemed to be a euphemism for a winning bet. Their credo ran, "Legally, I don't have to pay out anything and I don't intend to." The oldtime gypsies were just a laugh not a rip-off machine. And talking of machines, the modern acres of slot machines took in a lot more than they paid out. The SailorBoy wondered why there seemed to be no laws about this. If you printed money on your own press they jailed you for robbing the queen but if you ripped off the public by false claims – that was quite legal, apparently.

Dancing among the oldtime crowds in Old Seaside was a beautiful, young lady who reminded the SailorBoy of someone he had known a long time ago and yet not just someone but rather two or three old flames had somehow become one person who danced beside the sea in the twilight. But soon she disappeared in the crowds before the SailorBoy had a chance to get to know her. He cried after her, "Are you a ghost or a memory come alive?" But there was no answer as the scene from the old postcard slowly faded away.

The hawkers flogged their toys and gladrags. The freaks, fat or short or skinny or the bearded woman; all danced to the bands. Somewhere in the disappearing crowds, alas, was the young lady of days gone by. But all the ghosts of the past still come alive when the oldtime music plays. So play it again.

The Playscript

OUTLINE OF THE PLAY
ACT ONE -
WHEN THE OLDTIME MUSIC PLAYS
Scene One: Back in the Good Old Days
Scene Two: Wish You Were Here Again
ACT TWO -
THE MAGIC MILE AT THE CAFE
Scene One: Eat Your Fish & Chips and
Drink Your Tea
Scene Two: Seaside by the Sea
ACT THREE -
THE MAGIC MILE ON THE STRAND
Scene One: Boom, Boom, Boom
Scene Two: Dress a Little Less for More
ACT FOUR -
DANCINGGIRL FROM THE GOOD OLD DAYS
Scene One: The Old Postcard
Scene Two: See You Around

PRODUCTION NOTES
Stage time: full length musical of approximately
180-200 minutes.
Music
Eight songs and seven sets of verses for
recitation:
The Good Old Days;
Wish You Were Here Again;
The Fish and Chips Song;
Drink Your Tea;

Seaside Town;
Boom, Boom, Boom;
Dress A Little Less For More;
See You Around.

Actors
Eleven actors - five male, six female.
Age Groups
Suitable for all ages of actors and audience.
Set
One Set with two backdrops.
The basic scene is The Good Old Days Cafe
with the following backdrops:
(a) the Old Postcard and
(b) the Beach and Seaside of the Magic Mile.
Duration: A few weeks
Time Period: approximately the 1950s as
remembered today.
This grand production is recommended only for
those amateur groups who are experienced,
talented and well-equipped.

GENERAL STAGE INSTRUCTIONS
The Stage Setting for ALL Acts and Scenes
THE MAIN SET
The main set consists of an outdoor cafe in
the courtyard of a hotel overlooking the sea. The
cafe is separated by a rock wall from the
backdrop. (see separate stage instructions below)
The cafe consists of round tables, some with
umbrellas, lounge chairs, plants, shrubs, small

trees - as many as the stage can hold without disrupting the action or looking cluttered. There should be a clear path from left to right-stage for free movement of actors. This may be near the front-stage or may meander through the tables so long as it is wide and clear for stage movements including the parade in Act Three, Scene One.

SEAFRONT WALL

Downstage running the full length of the stage is a rugged stone wall about three feet high dividing the set from the backdrop. The set will remain the same throughout the play (with minor prop variations) but the backdrop will vary between the postcard of Old Seaside characters in Acts One and Three and the time warp Seaside Scenes (Act Two and Act Three).

BACKDROP NUMBER ONE - THE POSTCARD

Backdrop Number One - Postcard consists of the oldtime characters from 20s, 30s, 40s or 50s of Acts Two and Three plus the Lady of the Good Old Days. They are all dressed in period costumes and marching, strutting, jumping, dancing, etc., behind a Sergeant Major who is leading the procession and banging on his big drum. Immediately behind him and ahead of others comes a flute player and a Scot in kilts playing the bagpipes. All or most of these characters will "come alive" during the play - first the Lady in Act One (and later) then the rest of the paraders in Acts Two and Three. These characters should be painted larger than life-size, if possible, on a fairly dark background (e.g., blue or red or gray or brown).

Around all four sides of the backdrop there is a white band representing the borders of the postcard. Just below the top white band or border and running the full length of the postcard is the message in large script BEST WISHES FROM OLD SEASIDE. The bottom border of the postcard backdrop should be quite clear of the rocky wall of the seafront and indeed all four borders should be clearly seen by the audience.

BACKDROP NUMBER TWO - THE SEASIDE SCENE IN TIME WARP IN ACTS TWO OR THREE

The view is of the sea, beach and a pier in Old Seaside. The waterline runs from the bottom left corner to almost the top right corner in a semi-circle. In the top right corner is the big wheel with chairs and rides. From the top right to bottom right corner a pier runs from background to foreground. On the sands between waterline to the pier there are sunbathers, sandcastles, a pony, dogs, children, sun umbrellas, etc. On the sea there are waves, swimmers, small yachts. On the horizon there are low lying hills with a few clouds above. Top left the sun. On the pier there are promenaders, walking, gazing, taking photos, running, etc. All are in period costume (1920s, 30s, 40s, 50s). On the Big Wheel are chairs with patrons waving their arms and pointing.

CHARACTERS IN THE PLAY

ACTORS

Eleven actors, five men, six women, about six extras as bandplayers and passersby, fellow customers, servants. A chorus of 4-12+ for singing and dancing.

All characters, except the SailorBoy, are dressed in 20s, 30s, 40s or 50s period costume. The SailorBoy is dressed in a contemporary officer's uniform.

SAILORBOY: Principal Boy

A traveler returned to the scenes of his youth.

He is dressed in a SailorBoy suit and cap.

<u>The following characters who have stepped out of an old postcard:</u>

DANCINGGIRL: Principal Girl.

A young lady from the Good Old Days: A mysterious dancer who first stepped out of the old postcard.

SNOOTY: A drunken aristocrat, witty, affable and of mature years.

SKINNY: A tall, thin man.

VILLAIN LOTSADEBT: The Villain.

BILLBAILIFF: Pal of Lotsadebt

DAME KNOWITALL: The Grand Dame.

MILLIE/TILLIE: Seaside bleach blondes.

BEARDED LADY: A thin woman with a beard.

FAT WOMAN: A well-dressed, mature and stout woman.

Extras as band musicians, drummer, fluter and bagpiper as passersby, patrons in the cafe and background servants and miscellaneous paraders. Also dancers as a choir or chorus for backing in all eight songs or chorus.

ACT ONE
WHEN THE OLDTIME MUSIC PLAYS

SCENE ONE: BACK IN THE GOOD OLD DAYS
The scene opens in the garden of the Good Old Days Cafe, the outdoor garden of a hotel in Old Seaside - a British holiday resort. It is evening.

Front-stage is an outdoor garden-street cafe with a sign at left reading - The Good Old Days Cafe. The scene is partly lit, being evening time.

The backdrop (No. 1 - The Parade) and not yet visible, consists of a huge postcard with a white border all around. Within the border on a dark background is the picture of a parade in Old Seaside consisting of two or three bathing beauties, a drummer carrying a huge bass drum, a highland piper, a fluter, a bearded woman, a fortuneteller, followed by a villainous be-suited man, a thin man, a red-nosed drunk and a dancing-girl.

Patrons sit at various tables in the garden, front-stage – they may be extras, mannequins or painted props.

Enter from right-stage a sailor. He sits at a cafe seat front-stage and looks around with nostalgia as one who has been there before. He takes from his pocket and begins to examine a series of old postcards that bring back memories. Eventually he begins to stare at one of them in particular.

The lights dim as he remembers the old scene from the postcard while a thin spotlight focuses on the card in his hand. Then slowly the postcard/backdrop gradually lights up. It is the postcard showing the parade of oldtime seaside characters described above. The other lights dim somewhat, leaving the focus on the backdrop.

SailorBoy: Things have changed a lot after so many years. It's been a long time since I spent the evening in Old Seaside and I hear the music isn't the same. The people are different and where do their clothes and styles come from? London? New York? Paris? The worst places in the world. But it's not this place and not these people. And yet . . there was good music and good people back then.

Surely those old days were the good times? Am I drowning in a dread delusion of happy times that never really happened? No, I don't think so. *(he reshuffles the old postcards from his back pocket)* It seems that these old postcards prove my point. Slides and rides, beaches and bums, big wheels, sideshow freaks, dwarfs, bearded ladies, thin men, skinny drunken husbands and fat ladies - all were there.

He leaves his table, stands up and walks among the tables and chairs of the cafe, pensively and whimsically stepping lightly in front of the diners and dancers in the background. (inanimate props or live extras)

SailorBoy: People look so different today and it's not just the clothes or the hairstyles. No! It's something deeper than that. Their faces, eyes and bones are different and their inner person is somehow not quite the same. Why it's almost a different spirit.

They don't even play the same kind of music nowadays and what about the lifestyle? There's a whole lot more of help-yourself-ism and the values . . well . . are those really different now? *(shrugs)* One thing is certain, I don't feel as much at home here in Old Seaside. Maybe it's just that I've changed. But I ask myself, what was it really like back then?

Chorus/Dancers enter *as the music of* ***THE GOOD OLD DAYS*** *begins.*

SPECIFIC GUIDELINES for this scene - Act One - Scene One, the Chorus can be costumed as 1950s rock and roll dancers. One half of the dancers will be costumed as males and one half costumed as females with the Chorus providing vocal backup. The whole group emulates the dancing style of rock and roll in the 50s, both in paired and in line formation.

SailorBoy and the Chorus sing ***THE GOOD OLD DAYS***

THE GOOD OLD DAYS
Sung: Slow and Nostalgic

VERSE ONE:

  s fe s - l   s - m - d   m m - m   r *m* m
One of these days I'm going back to see Old Seaside
  s fe   s - l   s - m - d   r r - r d *r*
One of these days I'm gonna take it nice and slow
  r   m - m f - m m - m l_1
And just go drifting in and out
 l_1 m - m m m m - m   *r*
The places that I used to go
s s - l - s   m d   m   m - m
I may never find the same old crowd
  m   m   m - r f - m l_1
Where the oldtime music plays
 l_1 d r r r - d - r - d m   s   f   m
But I'd like to listen to the songs we sang then
  m - m   d - m   m *d*
Back in the good old days

VERSE ONE:
One of these days I'm going back to see Old Seaside
One of these days I'm gonna take it nice and slow
And just go drifting in and out
The places that I used to go
I may never find the same old crowd
Where the oldtime music plays
But I'd like to listen to the songs we sang then
Back in the good old days

REFRAIN:
One of these days I'm gonna find a place that plays it
Just like they used to play it many years ago
I'll listen again to the good old tunes
That thrill me, fast or slow
The good tunes that open up the past
In beautiful displays
I'd like to hear again the songs we sang then
One of these, one of these days

VERSE TWO:
Back in those days they were relaxed and cheerful people
Folks got to talking in a friendly sort of way
There was a casual kind of person then
That you rarely meet today
But if I could just walk down a street
Where the oldtime music plays
That good old music is enough to take me
Back to the good old days

SailorBoy: Old Seaside isn't all brash and bash, somewhat but not all. It's something more. Our old way of life was just hard work and good fun rewarded by a nice place at the seaside.

There was always the next bus and always another train coming along that old railway track. Anyhow, that's the way it seemed to me and the Good Old Days gave everybody more chances to be happy.

*SailorBoy repeats Verse Two of **THE GOOD OLD DAYS** as a solo, with only light vocal backing.*

VERSE TWO:
Back in those days they were relaxed and cheerful people
Folks got to talking in a friendly sort of way
There was a casual kind of person then
That you rarely meet today
But if I could just walk down a street
Where the oldtime music plays
That good old music is enough to take me
Back to the good old days

SailorBoy leaves left, followed by the Chorus.

Enter from right-stage, Villain Lotsadebt. He is a slick, smartly dressed salesman in a respectable dark blue suit, white shirt and red tie. He sports a gray, sleek moustache.

Villain Lotsadebt: Don't you worry old Sailorboy, I'll give you a reason to be happy again, ha, ha *(sarcastically)* with all my bargains and special deals. I'm Villain Lotsadebt. These people in Old Seaside don't know how I operate. I'll sell them something completely useless that they don't need and can't afford and when they've run up enough debt, they'll be ripe for peeling. *(imitates peeling something)* Then I'll set my old pal BillBailiff on them. He'll just love to seize all their possessions.

Lotsadebt, that's me, will get them and I'll get you lot out there as well. Just see if I don't. *(preens his moustache and chuckles menacingly)*

Audience: *(in unison)* Oh no you won't.

Villain Lotsadebt: Oh yes I will - just you watch me.

Audience: *(in unison)* Oh no you won't.

*As **Lotsadebt slinks offstage left**, he turns and sneers at the audience and shakes his fist at them before leaving.*

- Curtain -

ACT ONE
WHEN THE OLDTIME MUSIC PLAYS

SCENE TWO: WISH YOU WERE HERE AGAIN

The same set as in Act One, Scene One. The curtain opens on SailorBoy at the Seaside Cafe of the Good Old Days front-stage. However, the full set, including the large postcard of Old Seaside characters parading (see full description under Stage Setting) is mostly lit. He sings the first verse of **GOOD OLD DAYS.**

VERSE ONE:
One of these days I'm going back to see Old Seaside
One of these days I'm gonna take it nice and slow
And just go drifting in and out
The places that I used to go
I may never find the same old crowd
Where the oldtime music plays
But I'd like to listen to the songs we sang then
Back in the good old days

***Enter DancingGirl from the Good Old Days.** Preferably she is already on stage in an unlit area. Her 'entrance' is effected by the lights distracting attention from her by focusing on other parts of the set* *giving the impression of her sudden appearance from out of the postcard.*

She is dressed in somewhat oldtime style. She dances to the music and then joins in singing the refrain and second verse of ***GOOD OLD DAYS.***

DANCE NOTE

SailorBoy and DancingGirl dance to the theme song, either in rock and roll or traditional ballroom style in a fairly slow fashion. Music fades but they continue to dance slowly as . . .

SailorBoy: Who are you?

DancingGirl: I'm a girl from your dancing days.

SailorBoy: Where did you come from? You seemed to just appear.

DancingGirl: *(smiling)* Of course I just appeared, I'm from the Postcard. *(she points to a lady on the backdrop)* See this is me here. The music called me here. It's a special music you know, a magic melody. It brings back the past. As you sang yourself in the words of your song, it's one of those good tunes that open up the past and, truth spoken, here I am - a postcard appearance. A DancingGirl from the past!

They cease to dance.

SailorBoy: When I sang those words, I meant it as an image . . a figure of speech. It was a way of describing how I feel about oldtime music.

DancingGirl: Of course. But there's a personality in every old melody. The song we sang has a magic nostalgia, like a soldier's bugle call to summon the warriors to battle. A song can seem to roll back the curtains of time and call back the memories of the years. Don't worry, I may be from the past but it's still today, tonight. You haven't traveled in time - just in memory and perhaps in mood.

DANCE NOTE: *As they talk, SailorBoy and DancingGirl begin to dance again very slowly, far apart from each other in a formalized rock and roll style. Their fingers barely touch.*

SailorBoy: My memory of times past is vague.

DancingGirl: Yes, they may be just wishful memories.

SailorBoy: Perhaps if we got together with other oldtimers we could talk about the old times and separate the truth.

DancingGirl: *(slyly)* Most of the older people who remember those days are pretending to be young, dressing and painting and powdering and dying and wigging themselves and acting and prancing around just like the younger folks. *(pauses, finger on mouth)* There's no harm in that. One should try to stay young as long as possible, but it does seem as though most of the oldtimers have half forgotten the good old days.

SailorBoy: *(sadly)* And many others romanticize when they talk about their youth. They turn it into a legendary tale of romance or overcoming hardship and selling newspapers in bare feet. Ah, how they have overcome adversity. *(shakes his* *head in mock wonder)*

DancingGirl: *(less slyly but as one with a hidden purpose)* There must be oldtimers who still flourish somewhere. Perhaps old seaside vendors, beach bums, old brassbanders or freaks . . somewhere. *(whispers)* Perhaps on the Magic Mile where time has stood still up in that faraway seaside front. Some call it a time-warp where spirits of the past still live.

SailorBoy: *(pensively)* The Magic Mile? Where is it? Spirits of the past . . yes . . and are you alive or just a memory?

DancingGirl: *(cheerfully like someone accepting a challenge)* Let's dance and I'll show you the Magic Mile. There's only one thing that survives - that lives from Old Seaside.

SailorBoy: You mean memories?

DancingGirl: Well . . in a way yes but memories come and go and fade and we rewrite them every now and again . . I mean only one thing hard and fast and real and permanent that keeps our memories.

SailorBoy: What is it?

DancingGirl: A postcard - just an old postcard – that's all you really get to keep. *(she produces a postcard and hands it to SailorBoy)* It's not quite the same as the one you looked at earlier. So keep it close to your heart.

SailorBoy puts it in his left breast pocket.

DancingGirl: Yes, at the end of the day a postcard is all anyone ever gets from Old Seaside. Dreams fade. Romances fly away. Clothes wear out like us. Holiday money is all spent and the good food and drink is all consumed. What's left? Only vague and uncertain reminiscences, stories we change all the time.

But wait, maybe there is a souvenir or two, like an old postcard or an old photograph lying around in the dusty attic of our memories. That is the only real Old Seaside. It's a postcard that you and I can re-visit. It's still there – alive and real in a strange, out-of-the-way place that only I can show you. The Magic Mile is still there if only you have a magic guide, *(she points to her chest modestly and then bows to SailorBoy)* someone who knows, someone who can take you there, *(gently and pensively)* someone who can show you . . .

SailorBoy: *(puzzled)* Show me what?

DancingGirl: *(laughing)* Silly you. I'm trying to explain it and it's not easy. Let's see. I can show you a magic postcard and take you into the past along the Magic Mile. That's where I come from you know, *(points to backdrop)* that old postcard. And I can show you around there if you like, so that you can remember whether the good old days were really good or only old. You know, there are two kinds of oldies - Goldie Oldie and Moldy Oldie. See?

SailorBoy: Yes, of course and you can show me the Magic Mile from this old postcard. *(taps his heart)*

DancingGirl: *(smiling)* From the old postcard of your heart.

Dancing, they sing: **WISH YOU WERE HERE, AGAIN.** *Verses may be recited rather than sung. When music is irregular it may call for a trained voice. However, the decision whether to sing or recite is for the artist.*

The music of **WISH YOU WERE HERE AGAIN** *begins slowly and remotely, becoming just slightly faster and more audible as the song/dance sequence continues.*

Enter the Dancers/Chorus. *They are all dressed like the DancingGirl in oldtime dance costume. They dance at a slow/medium pace in the classic ballroom style, pairing briefly and then separating to form circles around the SailorBoy and DancingGirl.*

SailorBoy: *(as music and dance begin)* Your dancing is like a memory from the distant past.

WISH YOU WERE HERE, AGAIN
Sung: Slow and Nostalgic

VERSE ONE:

d   d - d t_1 d   r   d - l_1

Here's a postcard from Old Seaside

d   r   d   r   m   *d*

It says "Wish you were here"

f   f   m   f - f   s   f - m

O how the memories come alive

d   d - d   r   d s_1

Like starlight on the pier

d   d   d - t_1 d   r   d - l_1

Wish you were here in dear Seaside

d   r   d   r   m   m - d

With wind and waves on the strand

f   f   m   f - f   s   f   m

Wish you could join me sprayed and cool

d   d - d   m - m   f   *f*

A-walking along the sand.

REFRAIN:

d   d t_1 d   r   d - l_1 l_1

Yes, there's the white bright shining lights

d   r   d   r   m   d

And here's my keepsake pen

f   f   m   f   f   s - f   m

And now it writes Old Seaside nights

d   d   d   m   f   *f*

Wish you were here, again

d   d   d   m   f   *f*

Wish you were here, again

SEE YOU AROUND

VERSE ONE:
Here's a postcard from Old Seaside
It says "Wish you were here"
O how the memories come alive
Like starlight on the pier
Wish you were here in dear Seaside
With wind and waves on the strand
Wish you could join me sprayed and cool
A-walking along the sand.

REFRAIN:
Yes, there's the white bright shining lights
And here's my keepsake pen
And now it writes Old Seaside nights
Wish you were here, again
Wish you were here, again

VERSE TWO:
So I'm sending you some postcards
Just fun but true to life
There's red nosed drunk beneath a lamp
There's small guy with big wife
There's bearded lady, skinny man
Heartbroken lass in tears
There's giggling girls in crowds on crowds
Flowing by like years on years

REFRAIN:

*SailorBoy and DancingGirl
remain dancing as the lights dim.*

- Curtain -

ACT TWO
THE MAGIC MILE AT THE CAFÉ

SCENE ONE: EAT YOUR FISH AND CHIPS
AND DRINK YOUR TEA

The Good Old Days Cafe, as in Act One, has gone back in time and is now set on the Magic Mile - a magical one-mile strip of seafront set beside the old seaside. Changes in minor aspects of the set should be made to relate to the oldtime setting. For example, appropriate furniture and advertisements on the tables and walls and accessories such as plates, cups, glasses, handbags, cigarettes, pipes, potplant holders and jewelry.

*The music of the **Good Old Days** plays in the background as the curtain rises. The SailorBoy and DancingGirl are in a similar situation as at the end of Act One, Scene Two, dancing among the tables of the Good Old Days Cafe. The stage is in darkness and as the lights are gradually turned on, they reveal that the setting is now many years ago.*

Bespectacled Snooty the Drunk and Dotty the Bearded Lady are sitting at a table. Skinny Man in black and whites is clearing some tables. As the lights are brightened, the new backdrop - The Seaside Scene - is revealed and finally lit up intensively to express daytime and sunlight.

SailorBoy and DancingGirl look all around. She is pleased and happy with the self-satisfaction of one who has somehow brought about the magical change. She spreads her hands like a magician's assistant as one who says - See I told you so. She smiles. SailorBoy, by contrast, is astonished. He cannot believe what he sees. He stares at the backdrop and dashes around picking up and setting down oldtime objects in amazement.

SailorBoy: *(looking around)* Why it's daytime and in the same old hotel courtyard cafe the sun is shining. It's not . . it can't be . . and yet it is, judging by the decor, it's 50 years ago or more. How did we get here? Tell me, where are we?

DancingGirl: I told you I would show you around the Magic Mile where time has stood still and this is it - Old Seaside - many years ago. Everyone is here that you ever liked along the Magic Mile. No one good has gone anywhere. See, here's the Bearded Lady, *(pointing)* Old Dotty and the Red-Nosed Drunk, Snooty. *(she points at the drunk)* And there's the Thin Man waiting on tables *(pointing)* Big Skinny is his name and I'm sure the Beach-Bleached Blondes, Millie and Tillie, are somewhere here around and of course that Villain Lotsadebt. You'll need to watch your money when he's around the place.

SailorBoy: *(pleased and approaching the Bearded Lady)* It's true. Why it's Dotty and *(turning to Red Nosed Drunk)* Snooty. Why I heard you'd died? Didn't you die, my old chums?

Dotty and Snooty laugh.

Snooty is a gentleman who speaks in an upper-class British accent. His speech is slightly slurred. He is aristocratic and gangling in nature and mutters 'old chap' to himself at times and hiccups occasionally. He carries a more or less permanent glass of beer or wine and staggers and toasts the audience at times in a silent aside after some of his better lines.

Snooty: I was dead last night, old chap, dead drunk.

Dotty: *(shaking herself around and smiling)* No SailorBoy, my lad, I just came out here to the Magic Mile. I passed out the word that I was dead and gone so that certain folks I didn't like (for instance, Villain Lotsadebt) wouldn't come looking for me to pay them. You might say that the Magic Mile here is my own personal statute of limitations. I like it here.

Snooty: Same here chums. I just had to get away from those daft young chaps and gals and all that terrible noise they dance to. *(he winces)* This is where the good old music plays, here on the Magic Mile.

DancingGirl: *(to SailorBoy)* All you need to get to the Magic Mile is the key - the key of me. *(she points to herself brightly and dances around and sings)* Do, ray, me, mee. Hey, sit down SailorBoy.

SailorBoy perches on a table or on one of the higher chairs, still surveying the scene with amazement and pleasure.

SailorBoy: So this is where the oldtime music went - the Magic Mile - back in Old Seaside. Whad-e-ya-know!

Snooty: Let's all celebrate. *(to Skinny)* Waiter, do you have some tea? *(Skinny nods)* Well, do drink it sometime that's a good chap but bring us something stronger, eh? Ha, ha. How's about some beer, waiter?

Skinny: Cheers. That's decent of you. I'll have a Guinness.

Snooty: For me, for us, not you. Bring us some beer.

Skinny: *(reluctantly)* Oh, right you are, cock. Cor, what a hog.

Snooty: *(peeved)* How dare you refer to me as cock and hog. *(looking around)* What kind of place is this anyway - a farmyard? See here, this tablecloth is really quite dirty.

Skinny: *(unperturbed and unrepentant, almost bored)* Well cock, it's been there six months and no one else ever made any complaint. *(the others laugh)*
        Then to DancingGirl and SailorBoy.
Well, you farmyard freaks, what would you like? We've some nice duck. It's very fresh. I shot it myself just yesterday.

Dotty: Really?

Skinny: Yes, shot straight through the heart in mid-air. Saw it fall 300 feet.

Snooty: *(sneering)* You wasted your shot, Skinny. A fall like that would have killed it, anyway.

DancingGirl: We'll try some fish and chips waiter, thank you.

*Sailorboy and DancingGirl sing **THE FISH AND CHIPS SONG**.*

THE FISH AND CHIPS SONG
Sung: Fast

VERSE ONE AND REFRAIN:

s   d - d   m s d¹   t
O I'll have some fish and chips please
d¹ r¹   l - l - l - l
If that's all right with you
 f   r - r - r   f   t - t - t
Not too much grease - some mushy peas
l   s s s - f m
And salt and vinegar too
s   d - d m - s d¹ - d¹ t
No more the dainty dinner do
 d¹ r¹   l - l - l - l
No more them dunking dips
l s s - s s - t   t l
I say if it's all right with you
 s - s   s   f r   d
I'll have some fish and chips

VERSE ONE AND REFRAIN:
O I'll have some fish and chips please
If that's all right with you
Not too much grease - some mushy peas
And salt and vinegar too
No more the dainty dinner do
No more them dunking dips
I say if it's all right with you
I'll have some fish and chips

VERSE TWO:
Now the Admiral was in the pink
His ships were spiffy clean
Your Majesty what do you think?
He asks the blooming Queen
Says she I absolutely love
This fleet of men and ships
The only thing they need more of
Is good old fish and chips

VERSE THREE:
Well my Uncle Ray drops dead one day
We lay him down in flowers
Then we start a good wake right away
To brighten those sad hours
Ahh . . suddenly he bolts upright
And fear and terror grips . . .
We ask, What brought you back? He cried
I smell some fish and chips

VERSE FOUR: *(SailorBoy sings)*
See I knew a glamour girl I say
As pretty as the moon
Says she, Come visit me some day
So I showed up right soon
She asked, What would you like to do?
And smiled those lovely lips
I said, If it's all right with you
We'll have some fish and chips

VERSE FOUR: *(DancingGirl sings)*
See I knew a handsome man I say
As cheerful as the moon
Says he, Come visit me some day
So I showed up right soon
He asked, What would you like to do?
We've some nice river trips
I said, If it's all right with you
We'll have some fish and chips

***Enter Lotsadebt** stealthily and cunningly from left-stage followed by Grand Dame Knowitall who carries a large plastic bucket and spade.*

Lotsadebt: *(points at the others one by one)* You, £10 for your meal. You and you £15 each for your dinner and £20 for your drinks. Let's just round it up, say £100 each with special fees and interest. Okay?

Dame Knowitall: That's outrageous. How can you charge so much? Anyway what am I saying - what right have you to charge them anything? You don't even own this café. *(turning to others)* I just knew he was going to get up to his old tricks again. *(shakes her spade at him and chases him offstage)*

The others join in and shout after him.

Others: Out you moneygrabber. Beat it and don't come back. You'll get nothing from us. You're always looking for money.

Snooty: Anyway, that reminds me of my neighbors. Last year my yard flooded out with water and I appealed to them for some neighborly help. They advised me to keep ducks. Bad advice with trigger-happy chaps around like you, Big Skinny.

Big Skinny clearly ignores Snooty.

Dotty: *(to Skinny)* And some soup for me, Skinny.

Skinny: *(leaving stage right)* Certainly.

Snooty: I don't know why he ignores me like that. It's . . why . . it's class warfare. He hates me because I'm . . I'm. *(he puffs up his chest)*

Dotty: A drunken bum who's had too much to drink already.

Snooty: *(he smiles)* Yes exactly. *(frowns)* No, no. I'm a respectable chap. Why, I spent most of today looking for work or *(muttering aside)* or was it looking at work? Oh yes . . some men were digging up the road for a burst water-pipe.

Dotty: *(outraged)* Don't tell me you were looking for work, you bum. I saw you coming out of the pub earlier.

Snooty: *(resignedly)* Well, I had to come out sometime.

Dotty: But . . you were half drunk.

Snooty: Half drunk yes. I know. I'm sorry. I ran out of money. That's why I

had to leave. They wouldn't let me sleep there. *(he brightens)* But I got some later from pater. Good old dad. *(he closes and opens his eyes lazily)*
> *He addresses SailorBoy.*
Pardon me, sir. *(he squints and shakes his head, pointing at the sky).* Is that the sun or the moon behind those hazy clouds?

SailorBoy: *(cheerfully)* I have no idea, sir. *(spreads his arms wide)* I'm only a visitor in town.

Snooty: O beg your pardon - no offence, sir. *(touches his head to steady it)*

DancingGirl: *(laughing heartily)* Oh, the wit is flying, *(to SailorBoy)* I haven't laughed so much since Old Dog was a pup.

Dotty: *(laughing)* Since Big Ben was a watch. Ho, ho.

SailorBoy: *(to Snooty)* What brings an upper-class brat like you to Old Seaside anyway, mate?

Snooty: Listen chum, same three things as anyone else. Most chaps come to Old Seaside for three things. A girl, a change and a rest but do they get'em? Well, a change, a girl or a rest, I mean. Well, maybe! But mostly it seems like the cafes pick up the change, the other fellow gets the girl and you feel so bad the bartenders get the rest.

Dotty: Here. Ain't it the truth, cock?

Snooty: Ma'am, please watch your language. I'll have you know that my brother is a peer.

Dotty: Oh, a pier. *(puzzled)* That's the thing that sticks out there in the sea. People walk all over and jump on and spit on it?

Snooty: *(defensively)* Oh, that was only in his wild and exotic youth, ma'am. He's quite a straight . . straightforward chap nowadays. Look, I say, here comes Big Skinny with the refreshers. Good Old Skinny. Good lad, Skinny.

Enter Skinny with soup, fish and chips and beer on a tray. He places the beer on Snooty's table, the fish and chips for SailorBoy and DancingGirl and soup for Dotty. Snooty frowns at the beer. Dotty peers into soup and seems amazed.

Dotty: *(romantically gazing into the air)* Ah, indeed, the lock of a child's hair can bring back *(she sighs)* such fond memories *(she shakes her head dreamily)* of loving and romantic girlhood. Still, *(she recovers from her memories sharply)* still, *(to Skinny, petulantly)* I'd prefer not to find hairs in the soup, waiter! *(points to her soup disgustedly)*

Skinny: *(disbelieving, looks at her soup closely, looks at her and answers stiffly)* Ma'am that's not a child's lock of hair. *(coldly)* Ma'am that is the reflection of your beard!

Dotty: *(relieved)* Oh, is that all. Please forgive me, ho, ho, beg pardon. My beard is my fortune you know, can't complain about that . . .

Waiter looks down at Snooty frowning into his beer.

Skinny: *(to Snooty)* Something wrong, bloke?

Snooty: This is a very small beer. It says it costs three pounds in the menu - that can't be the three pound glass of beer.

Skinny: Why not?

Snooty: It's too small.

Skinny: That'll be all the less for you to hold in your hand, mate. Three quid, if you please. Pay now or later.

Snooty: *(grudgingly handing over the money)* I'd better go outside for a breath of fresh air – it's all I can afford. On second thoughts, three quid it is and here's a penny tip for you, my good man.

Skinny: *(outraged)* A penny tip. Why you stingy old glasshopper.

Snooty: *(imitating Skinny in a crude Seaside accent)* All the less for you to count, cock! *(chuckles to himself)*

Skinny: *(displeasingly and dryly)* Ha, ha. Things are so expensive these days. An older chap can't even afford a mid-life crisis. I remember the time when every Tom, Dick and Harry could have a jolly good mid-life crisis - blondes and all thrown in but not today.

Snooty: Hmm. Talk about inflation - high prices – that's what I like about Old Seaside - the only thing that's low is the ladies dresses. Oh, of course, the ethics of the waiters also, they're low too. I almost forgot about that . . .

Skinny: I'll thank you not to make remarks on waiter's honesty, mate. I'd have you know that we be fair and honest and give good service and treat customers decently.

Snooty: Really? *(thinks about it)* Decent? Do you keep the Golden Rule, Skinny?

Skinny: *(scratching his head)* Keep what?

Snooty: The Golden Rule.

Skinny: *(slightly puzzled)* I'm sure we do, cock. Do you drink it straight or with a tonic, eh?

Snooty: *(sprawling hopelessly in his chair and shaking his head)* And I'm the one whose supposed to be drunk. Look, old chap, can you give me a wake-up call in the morning?

Skinny: We don't do that, sir. But I'll get you a bottle of yeast tablets.

Snooty: Yeast tablets? What for?

Skinny: You eat 'em all mate and that way you're sure to rise up early in the morning. See? You'll be the talk of the town.

Skinny turns his back on Snooty who becomes annoyed.

Snooty: I can see you're making a fool of me.

Skinny: No point in that, cock. Your mum and dad already did that for you when you were born.

Skinny turns away and talks the others.
Is everything all right, mates?
Soup good Dotty?
To SailorBoy as Snooty looks puzzled.
I seem to have seen you here before, a long time ago, mate?

SailorBoy: Yes, I remember, it was back in the Good Old Days.

DancingGirl: *(recites or sings)*
Ah, the British upper classes.
The British upper classes
Are a bunch of snobby asses
But there's one thing in which they all excel
And that is talking rubbish and confusion
While creating the illusion
That they're really talking common sense quite well
What wonders a posh accent can achieve

SailorBoy:
Course number one
At upper class school
Is how to rule and how to fool
By using well accented drool

How to pull the blinding wool
Over the eyes by blabbing lies
Dressed up to sound
So true and clear
Into the victim's eager ear

DancingGirl:
The snobby upper classes seem so suave
While robbing you of everything you have
The taxman is their axeman you'll agree
They can be quite repressive
(in a posh accent)
But by gad they're so impressive
When they talk about their reverence for tea
Oh tea, yes tea
Do step up old boy and have a jolly old cup of tea
What wonders a posh accent can achieve.

Skinny: *(wakening up)* Hooray for the British upper classes.

All join together in reciting or singing
DRINK YOUR TEA.

DRINK YOUR TEA
Sung: Jolly

VERSE ONE:

d   d   d   d l_1 - d
Don't get scared or skittish
f   f   f   r - f
Fight to the finish
d   d   d d   r - d
Be proud to be British
d l_1 s_1
Drink your tea
d   d   d   d l_1 - d
No matter how you suffer
f   f   f   f   r - f
Keep a true stiff upper
f   f   f   f   m - m
Eat a good fish supper
f   s   f
Drink your tea

DancingGirl:
Don't get scared or skittish
Fight to the finish
Be proud to be British
Drink your tea

SailorBoy:
No matter how you suffer
Keep a true stiff upper
Eat a good fish supper
Drink your tea

Skinny:
Don't let worries hook you
Don't let life rebuke you
Let's all go cuckoo
Drinking tea, drinking tea
(to Snooty) You've a cheek to say - drink your tea. You never touch the stuff.

Snooty: I never said I did. I said you - not me - *(hic)* drink your tea. It's good enough for you, old boy.

DancingGirl:
Let's not get flappie
Let's not be snappy
Let's all be happy
Drink your tea.

Skinny:
Now working lads and lasses
Never fear the asses
Of the upper classes
Drinking tea, drinking tea

Snooty:
Fight them to the finish
Don't get scared or skittish
Remember we're British
Drink your tea, drink your tea

Skinny: Drink thy brew, lad.

- Curtain -

ACT TWO
THE MAGIC MILE AT THE CAFÉ

SCENE TWO: SEASIDE BY THE SEA

*The scene opens to the music of **SEASIDE TOWN**. The scene is the same seaside hotel outdoor cafe overlooking the beach. The plants and other props may be changed or moved around to indicate that time has passed since the last scene or even that the action takes place in a similar but not the same scene. Tillie and Millie, large beach-bleached blondes in bikinis or similar beachwear, are sitting at tables laughing and chattering.*

Dame Knowitall, marches briskly on stage from left *carrying a large empty plastic bucket and a spade. She is a darkly made-up lady, plump and wearing a turban and eastern-type robes. She is a fortuneteller by trade. She leans over the rock wall to address a crowd gathered below on the beach. This crowd may be visible on stage if extras are available or may be identifiable by voice only. Dame*

Knowitall carries a crystal ball and places it beside her. She is partly turned away from the audience but turns to the side to consult the crystal.

Dame Knowitall: *(to audience)* Hello everybody. I'm Grand Dame old Knowitall. That gentleman there, you on the beach down there beside the pony, yes you with the diamond rings and gold watch and silver chain. I'll tell you your fortune.

Voice from Crowd: What?

Dame Knowitall: I'll tell you your fortune love. *(aside - to audience)* Better still, I'll take it from you for safekeeping.

She rubs her hands acquisitively.
Derisive laughter comes from the crowd.

Dame Knowitall: Yes I foresee a wicked, dark lady who'll try to steal it from you, love. *(thinks)* Yes, I see her fascinated by your wealth - gee, what am I saying? That may be me. You love, you in the baggy bags, I can see that you've enough money saved up to do you till the day you die.

Voice from Crowd: Who, me? You're a silly pollock.

Dame Knowitall: Yes, you have chum, you've enough cash to do you till the day you die or next Thursday - whichever comes first. *(howls and jeers come from the crowd)* So, prove me a liar by dropping dead penniless before then if you wish - I don't mind. Here, let me look into my crystal ball again. *(she peers into the ball)* Terrible. I foresee a storm. Lawd, it's freezing and bitter. The wind howls, it's a real brass monkey's nightmare. The waves beat on the shore. Yes, it's c-o-o-old. The shivers run down my spine. *(she draws her collar around her)*

Voice from Crowd: All right, when's the storm coming?

Dame Knowitall: When? How should I know? Ah, that is to say, the spirits do not reveal that. *(she turns to an assistant offstage)* Hey you, shut off that draught – you're giving me false prophesy. Close that gate. *(shivers)*

Voice from Crowd: I know you - you're really a blonde underneath. You're just a phony.

Dame Knowitall: Why are you a full-time layabout, a dropout?

Voice from Crowd: I'm not. It's just that I've got a bum job - bumming - get it?

Dame Knowitall: There's a lady out there who loves baking, right? *(aside - to audience)* Surely that's a safe guess?

Woman's Voice: Yes I do. That's me.

Dame Knowitall beams with success.

Woman's Voice: Yes, I just love baking because it makes my hands so white and clean.

Dame Knowitall: *(tapping her head)* Ah, I can foresee a tragedy.

Woman's Voice: What is it – what's in my future?

Dame Knowitall: Ahh, I regret that someone in your poor family is about to die of food poisoning. *(howls from the crowd)* Now let me see, yes I foresee, Punch over there is going to kill his wife Judy.

> *(more howls of derision come from the crowd as paper cups and food are thrown at her)*

Oh forget it! Visit my tent on the pier if you want to hear any more. Oh, I give up. Why should I try to foretell the future?

> *(turning to the blondes)* Girls, it's so difficult, you wouldn't believe it. It's hard enough to find out what happened last night, without trying to find out about the future.

> *(she pats her turban thoughtfully)* Maybe I'll just look around for an easier profession. *(considers)* I can't think of one - after all, all professions have their ups and downs.

***Enter Snooty from right-stage** and staggers up behind Dame Knowitall and pulls off her turban, revealing blonde hair underneath.*

Snooty: Everybody knows that you're just an old phony.

Dame Knowitall: What's wrong with a northern blonde anyway and what's so fascinating about the mysterious south and east? Why is an eastern look supposed to be psychic? Give me the good Old Seaside anyday.

Snooty staggers off stage-left still holding her turban in his hand.

Dame Knowitall: *(she shouts after him)* Hey, just a minute - give me back my turban.

Snooty throws it back to Dame Knowitall who hits it into the air with the spade and catches it in the bucket.

Millie: *(shaking blonde hair)* Never mind him. He's always drunk and talks a lot of rubbish anyway. I like it here in Old Seaside - even if the gypsies are phonies.

Tillie: Me too. I ain't going out east or down south anytime soon - fortuneteller or not.

Dame Knowitall: Well, it's not a good way to earn a living, but it's better than working for Big Brother Boss. There's no such thing as a good job, you know. You need to have a self-employed profession like me. *(lamely)* Well, I'm a fortuneteller. *(brightening)* What is your profession? *(looking at each of the girls in turn as they remain blank)* What do you do for a living?

Millie: *(deadpan)* As little as possible.

Tillie: *(deadpan)* Me too, I try to avoid the boss.

Dame Knowitall: Well, you're both on the wrong track. Never work for a boss. There's no such thing . . .

Millie: You told us . . as a good job.

Dame Knowitall: Yes, or a good boss.

Tillie: Yes, we agree. But still you've got to do something for a living.

Dame Knowitall: Well? Other than as little as possible, what do you do for a living - if that's not an embarrassing question?

Millie: Well actually *(looks at her nails)* I'm working up in the new morgue on Layton Road.

Dame Knowitall: The where?

Millie: The new morgue - the mortuary.

Dame Knowitall: *(she stares and looks horrified)* How nice.

Millie: Yes, next time you're up that way just drop in.

Dame Knowitall: *(feeling her throat and gulping)* Well, I'll try . . . I mean I'll try not to.

Tillie: And I work for Clemondo, the hairdresser. *(she shakes her head and twists up her nose as at a bad smell)* O he's a strange one - really a weirdo.

Dame Knowitall: I know – don't tell me - I went there once for a hairdo. He says, ma'am do you want gas or an injection? I say what - for a hairdo? Is that perm machine safe? Oh, yes, he says, it's safe all right. I thought maybe, he says, you wanted the warts removed. What warts? I was outraged. I have no warts. How dare you? What about this, he says and tweaks my nose like this. *(she tweaks her nose)* I walked out and never went back. Once a lady gets over 40, the insults start flying.

Tillie: You're right, he ain't a good boss. He keeps offering me gas or injections too. I don't know why! You know, talking about fortunetelling, I once dreamed that my great-aunt was dead. Three days later it proved true. I tried the same dream on my boss *(shrugs hopelessly)* but it didn't work . . . *(spreads her hands helplessly)* All you can do is try.

Millie: *(in a matter-of-fact gossipy tone)* Most bosses run the firm on their wits, that's why there's so many business bankruptcies. My last boss was an undertaker – that's where I got the experience for my promotion to the mortuary. Anyway, in the undertakers it was so lonely – no body cared.

Dame Knowitall: *(interrupting with much sympathy)* Taking a way-out job like that was a grave mistake. There's no such thing . . . *(she pauses and starts looking over the parapet)*

Millie: Now where was I?

Anxious to resume her gossipy tale.

Millie: Oh yes . . . No such thing, you know, as a good job. Anyway when the undertaker, my boss, took sick, the doctor said the only hope for him was to be sent to a warmer climate. I said to the doctor, if you want to send him to a warmer climate, you do it yourself - I don't want no part of that kind of thing. No, he says, he didn't mean down there *(points down to floor)* he only meant a nice place with warmer weather. So we sent him way down south to sunny Sutherland.

Dame Knowitall: But that's way up north in cloudy freezing Scotland.

Millie: I know but it sounds southern, it ought to be southern. It's ridiculous that a place up north should be called Sutherland, anyhow. We all could really and truly plead ignorant of geography. Naturally, he died up in Sutherland. I mean he died naturally.

Tillie: What did he die of?

Millie: *(dumbly)* Of a Friday. Friday is a very unlucky day . . almost everybody dies of a . . .

Tillie: *(interrupting)* I mean, what was the complaint?

Millie: No complaint. Everybody was happy except him that died.

Dame Knowitall: I don't get it. What if all your bosses died, you'd only get another boss. You'd be no better off.

Millie: Yes, I would be better off. The new boss couldn't guess right away where I hide on the job. *(screwing up her nose impishly)* Now where in all the hiding places in a morgue do you think I could hide?

Dame Knowitall: Oh, that's a stiff choice. *(points at Tillie, rolls her eyes and shakes her head, then aside to audience)* What some people will do to avoid an honest day's work. If you like I'll help YOU to find a nice place of rest in the beach. *(she pretends to scoop up sand with her spade)*

Millie and Tillie both look bored and uninterested during the following monologue.

Dame Knowitall:
But it's true
There's no such thing as a good job
Every boss I ever knew
Was just a no good slob
Living on other people's money
While we bog down in debt
You slave your guts out
While the boss just struts out
You do your best like a bee making honey

And what thanks do you get?
No matter now much you slave and save
You never have enough money it seems
To buy that little farm with charm
That brings alive your dreams
The boss acts like a kindly king
Behind his back he hides his sting
He'll only rip you off and rob
Believe me gals, there's no such thing
As a good job
(in summary) So be self-employed like me.
Do what you're good at and be yourself.

Millie and Tillie look at each other and shrug. They are still bored. They yawn conspicuously and tap their yawns languidly and long with the tips of their elegantly manicured hands.

Millie: *(to Dame Knowitall, languidly)* You're one to talk about doing what you're good at. You couldn't predict the date tomorrow much less tell the future.

Dame Knowitall: Well, I'm just an entertainer really. It's only fun and flattery . . . Nobody expects me to foretell the future, really.

Enter Villain Lotsadebt carrying a briefcase, dressed in a business suit, white shirt, red tie, waistcoat, polished dark shoes, short hairstyle with sleek moustache. He wears glasses and looks very professional, speaks well, quickly and smoothly.

Lotsadebt: *(racily)* Ladies. I'm from the Rent-A-Brother-in-Law Agency of Seaside-on-Sea.

Dame Knowitall: *(in disbelief)* Rent a what?

Lotsadebt: *(more slowly and clearly)* A Brother-in-Law.

Millie and Tillie shake their heads in disbelief.

Dame Knowitall: It's a new insurance racket.

Lotsadebt: No ma'am, we really can provide you with a rented out brother-in-law at very competitive rates.

Millie: You're joking!

Tillie: You're the jester from the circus!

They laugh but Lotsadebt looks annoyed and offended.

Lotsadebt: Now just a minute ladies. Don't let my lack of height arouse your stereotypical prejudice against short persons. *(adamantly)* First, hear me out.

> *The others shrug boredly, suppress giggles. Dame Knowitall fixes her eyelashes, Millie examines her toes and Tillie her fingernails.*

Dame Knowitall: O don't let us stop you. *(taps her head towards the others and shrugs again)*

Lotsadebt: And I'm not mad either. Listen, we can rent you out the most undeserving, dirty brother-in-law you ever saw with at least four days growth of beard. Rarely uses your bath but is guaranteed to overflow it within three days.

Dame Knowitall: Stop right there. How can he overflow the bath if he hardly ever uses it?

Lotsadebt: Anything destructive - he always does it somehow. He also provides his own beer, empties the fridge within a week, sleeps on your couch half the day and roams around banging and bumping all night, jams your window open, breaks the lock on at least one of your cabinets, smashes several valuable items and always goes out without locking your front door.

Lotsadebt begins to laugh hysterically at his sales-speel and twirls his false moustache.

Lotsadebt: The most typical brother-in-law you ever had - all yours *(to Dame Knowitall)* or yours *(to Tillie)* or yours ma'am *(to Millie)* at our special introductory offer of only 50 pounds a week plus couch and board or 15 pounds a day delivered alive, to your back door, at no extra cost.

Millie: *(puts her hands in her ears and shouts)* Stop it. I can't stand it anymore.

Tillie: Yes, I agree with Millie. This is too much.

Lotsadebt: Listen, even better news, 10% of all you pay in rent for your very own homewrecker is paid to the International Foundation for Family Values.

Dame Knowitall: Stop, stop STOP - this is lunacy. What on earth makes you think that I or any other sane person would want a brother-in-law – it's the last thing I ever wanted for Christmas?

Tillie and Millie stare wide-eyed at Lotsadebt and look mystified, spread their hands at each other and tap their temples.

Lotsadebt: *(to Dame Knowitall)* That's the point. *(excited and smiling)* You've hit the nail on the head.

Dame Knowitall: *(mystified)* I have?

Lotsadebt: *(with great enthusiasm)* Yes, the brother-in-law is the most neglected family member, don't you see? That's why true family values require us to treat him with care and respect. Husbands and wives mostly put up with each other. Everybody just loves the kiddies and the grandpas and grandmas are practically hero-worshipped. But the brother-in-law is so neglected that he often can't find a home anywhere.

Millie: He won't find one with me.

Tillie: *(nodding towards Lotsadebt)* I do believe he's serious you know.

Millie: I know he is − that's what's beginning to bother me.

Lotsadebt: Believe me, we all deserve a brother-in-law and every brother-in-law deserves a home. *(sniffs with exaggerated but apparently genuine concern)* Ladies, seaside resorts are just coming down with penniless brothers-in-law with no one's couch to sleep on . . believe me.

Dame Knowitall: Oh, I believe you alright. *(seriously)* There's probably a million of the poor unwanted bums out there.

Lotsadebt: Then you all want one?

Millie: Now that's where you're wrong, they may be out there but I don't need one. If there's one thing I don't need, it's a bum sleeping on my couch at night. But if I did I could get one free but not me.

Dame Knowitall: Nor me.

Tillie: Nor me, Lotsadebt, no way.

Dame Knowitall: Will you get this into your thick little skull . . I don't want one . . not to rent, not to buy, not even to try on approval or on consignment or on lease or any other way.

Lotsadebt: Oh yes, I forgot; you can have one for five hours free on consignment, that is on approval or return to the agency or *(desperately)* our special two for the price of one coupon.

Tillie: *(becoming outraged)* Will you get lost Lotsadebt? Beat it. You and your family values, two for the price of one racket.

Millie: Yea, vamoose.

Dame Knowitall merely rolls her eyes in agony.

Tillie: What is this place - a lunatic asylum?

Enter DancingGirl along with SailorBoy, overhearing the conversation.

DancingGirl: No, it's just good old Seaside by the Sea.

SailorBoy: *(laughs)* What's the matter?

Millie: Well, here I was sitting here practicing my artistic talents, doing my own toenails, getting a bit of sun and all of a sudden this dwarf dashes up and tries to sell me a brother-in-law. What's going on here? That's the last thing I need.

Lotsadebt: Rent - not sell - rent. Rent in the interests of family values.

Millie: *(outraged)* What's the difference? What sort of place is this anyway? I thought this place was respectable?

They all laugh.

SailorBoy: Respectable - never! It's just Seaside by the Sea. The funniest things happen here, you know.

DancingGirl: *(to SailorBoy)* Exactly, it's just as I told you. See, here's the Magic Mile in full swing: a phony fortuneteller, two bleach blondes trying hard to think but never quite succeeding and a villain who rents out brothers-in-law for a living. Whacky eh? This is Old Seaside, alright?

Lotsadebt shrugs as one who has tried his best and can accept his failure.

Lotsadebt: *(apologetically he rubs his hands with cunning and hypocritical ingratiation)* The company has me on commission only basis. That's why I try so hard. They said I could make a fortune cause no one else was flogging them. I guess it's ridiculous. I'm sorry ladies. *(he bows)*

Millie: Oh forget it Lotsadebt. Most people would do just anything for a living, especially Tillie there.

Tillie: *(outraged)* Oh no, that's not true! I would never murder anyone.

DancingGirl: *(pensively and shaking her head at the two girls)* Yes, it's weird but there are funny things in other far-off places too. I've traveled the world and seen wonders. In Spain, they chase the bulls and keep the girls within rails. With us it's the opposite. In gay Paree, the little kids drink wine and in the cradle of civilization along the Nile I've seen nothing more civilized than crocodiles. There are also some very strange sights in old Amsterdam.

SailorBoy: I know but you can kinda count on those faraway places being strange but here in Old Seaside you really know what to expect.

(he joins in reciting or singing SEASIDE TOWN):

SEASIDE TOWN*
Sung: Jolly

VERSE ONE:

   d   d   f   s   l - s - f
Y'all come down to Seaside Town
  f - s   f   r   d
Seaside by the Sea
   d l_1 d   f   l - l   s   f
Along the strand and over the sand
 f s   f   m   f   s
Is all the fun you need
   d l_1 - d r - *f* f s   l - l   s   *f*
Some love to go to the slopes of snow
   f - f - s - f   r   d
Seems kind of cold to me
  r - d - r - m - *f*   s   l   s   *f*
But boats are afloat with friendly folk
 f - s - r   m   d   *f*
In Seaside by the Sea

* *(or any other seaside resort)*

REFRAIN
d l_1 - d   r - f f   s   1 - 1   s f
So skid in the snow, or climb high or low
d l_1 - d   r - f f   s   1 - 1   s f
Let the big city lights bring you flutters and frights
   f - f - s - f   r - r   d
Fly south till you catch a flee
r - r - d - r - m - f s   1   s f
But that's not the way we pass the day
  r - r - d - r - m - f s   1   s f
And that's not quite how we spend the night
  f - s - r   m   d f
In Seaside by the Sea

Tillie:

I come from Seaside Town
Seaside by the Sea
Down the strand and along the sand
Is all the fun I need
I really don't know what they see in the snow
Seems kinda cold to me *(shivers)*
So while I'm alive, I'll jump and jive
In Seaside by the Sea

SailorBoy:

So skid in the snow, climb high or low
Let the big city lights bring you flutters and frights
Fly south till you catch a flee
But that's not quite how we spend the night

Millie and All:
And that's not the way we pass the day
In Seaside by the Sea

SailorBoy:
There are sights and sounds and tastes abound
In the mists of memory
The soft ice-cream is a beautiful dream
There's a nice old pot of hot tea
And there is no gloom in the oyster room
It's all cockles and mussels for me

Dame Knowitall: Or smack your lips on the fish and chips.

SailorBoy: Sounds mighty good to me.

DancingGirl: In Seaside by the Sea

Lotsadebt:
Oh I come from Seaside Town
Seaside by the Sea

SailorBoy:
O we used to float on a wobbly boat
And paddle and dive and cry
O the old ship's bell and the salty smell
Of the seaweeds a-swirling by

But there's a place where the good old days
Are still alive to me
It's down along with my pals and gals
Down beside the old seaside
In Seaside-by-the-Sea

DancingGirl:
O come on girls, SailorBoy and you too, Lotsadebt, let's all go down to the beach and hear the brass band.

All: In Seaside by the Sea.

All leave left-stage, except the Villain.

Lotsadebt leans backwards and shouts at the audience after the others have gone.

Lotsadebt: Don't worry I'll get their money yet.

Audience: *(in unison)* No! No! No! Boo. Boo. Boo.

Lotsadebt: Oh yes I will.

Audience: *(in unison)* Oh no you won't.

Lotsadebt: And I'll get your money too.

Audience: *(in unison)* Boo-oo-oo.

- Curtain -

ACT THREE
THE MAGIC MILE ON THE STRAND

SCENE ONE: BOOM, BOOM, BOOM

The scene is the same but the action moves more forward and left of center, towards the strand surrounding the café. (Large-scale productions and movies may create a separate set that differs from Act Two).

Dame Knowitall, Tillie and Millie, Lotsadebt, SailorBoy and DancingGirl are returning one and two at a time from the beach to the café's outer tables away from the bar and nearer the passersby where they are joined by Snooty, Skinny and the Fat Lady. Later they celebrate with a song as the band arrives and passes through on its way down the strand.

Enter SailorBoy and DancingGirl.
They dance center-stage.

DancingGirl: I told you that I could show you the good old days here on the Magic Mile where time has stood still and people are just as good as they were back then.

SailorBoy: And all our favorite people are still around. I should have known that there's somewhere where the good people go and just carry on forever. There's lots of fun and a sense of, "Hey, what's going on?"

DancingGirl:

Fun people are always looking for something new
It seems as though the good folks of long ago
Were always ready for a date
Ready to have a pint with a mate
Ready to lend a willing hand
And stroll with you arm and arm along the strand
Quick to laugh, to try, to strive,
To build each other up
And not let life tear each other down
To share a friendly cup
To joke and be a clown
To make new hope drive out the old dismays
Ah, it was fun to be alive
Back in the good old days

SailorBoy:

And fun to be with you
I'm one of the lucky few
Who like the pretty girls
The girls who rarely get the whirls

DancingGirl: *(puzzled)* But surely all men like the pretty gals?

DancingGirl dances gracefully around stage while the SailorBoy gives his monologue.

SailorBoy:
Not so, oh dear no, and as for you
You really ought to know
For you were available when I came along
And you're as pretty as a summer song
It's always the pretty girls
Who never get the dates
It's always the plain Janes
Who have a dozen keen aspiring and hot breathing mates
Most men prefer ugly women

DancingGirl: *(stopping her dance briefly, puzzled)* Why? But why?

SailorBoy:
I don't know why
Maybe most men are afraid of beauty
Because it's not in their soul
Or maybe they like to hide away in a guilty little hole
Like silly little boys at heart

Who make the good girls cry
But me, I'm different, I'm a freak, I always try
To date the prettiest girl around
You wouldn't believe the lovely beauties I've found
In all my ports of call
Believe me, the girl
Who doesn't get the whirlwind swirl
Who doesn't even have a date
Is usually the most beautiful one of all
Now for example take my date
I now have you. Yes, you. Yes, you
(he throws out his arm in joy)
I do like pretty ladies
What a freakish fate
That makes me one of the fortunate few
For you
Are prettier than any queen
See what I mean?

DancingGirl: *(stopping her dance and thoughtfully approaching the SailorBoy and speaking musingly)*
Well, what you say does seem to make some sense
Really, I've seen
How strange men are
I've seen beautiful women, with fine

spirits, deserted for
Obnoxious harridans
There's truth in what you say
O what a life

> *DancingGirl and SailorBoy sit down
> at one of the tables.*

SailorBoy: Still here on the Magic Mile I think people are more fun loving and happier and decent than . . .

Enter Lotsadebt strutting as before, holding his briefcase . . and followed by Millie, Tillie, Dame Knowitall (in full turban and gear), Fat Lady, Skinny and Snooty, all coming back from the beach, slightly wet and carrying dripping bathing costumes which they wring out, hold up and put aside conspicuously.

Lotsadebt: What was that about the people nowadays?

SailorBoy: Well, we agreed that while men were mighty peculiar critters in their dealings with women, still and all, most people are good and decent here on the

Magic Mile.

Lotsadebt: *(incredulous)* You mean today. In this day and age most people are good and decent and always pay their way?

DancingGirl: Of course.

Lotsadebt: *(slapping his knee)* Now how wrong can you be? Why we're all a bunch of no-good layabouts and I personally deeply resent being thought of as decent or good or kindly or anything silly like that. *(to others)* What do ya say?

Others: Oh yes. We agree with you Lotsadebt. Lotsadebt's right.

Lotsadebt: Really SailorBoy, you ought to know better. Listen. I was just down on the beach there riding on a pony. Now I ask you was that pony surefooted? *(scans faces of DancingGirl and SailorBoy)*

SailorBoy: *(shrugs)* Well, was he?

Lotsadebt: Sure, he was surefooted. He threw me on the sand and kicked me three times in the same place. *(holds his back in agony)*

SailorBoy: But that was only a dumb animal.

Lotsadebt: Come on, who do you think trained him - another horse?

SailorBoy: Oh well, think of all the good things here in old seaside . . .

Lotsadebt: Good things. I just lost a good umbrella down on the beach, there.

SailorBoy: So you forgot it? Right?

Lotsadebt: Wrong. The owner saw it and recognized it as his own!

DancingGirl: *(teasingly)* You know what they say - If you want to lose your troubles and debts put them in your umbrella! Anyway, it wasn't your own umbrella. I still say people here on the Magic Mile are the kindest and most decent in the world.

Millie: Talking about debts, that reminds me how horrible people are. I agree with Lotsadebt. Why, I'm so deeply in debt and the good book says the borrower is the slave of the lender. I must get out of it.

DancingGirl: Yes, get out of debt.

Millie: Oh no, that's impossible. I need to get out of town.

Tillie: Before you go, give me back the watch you stole last night. Come on now. I've no time to spare.

Millie hands over her watch. Snooty dashes in from right-stage, half drunk, looks around, staggers, falls over.

Snooty: Where's the loopy? Where's the loo?

Dame Knowitall: *(elegantly pointing to left-stage).* Follow the smell . . smell's the clue.

Snooty dashes around again, turns full circle and dashes out left-stage.

Fat Lady: Oh, I agree with Lotsadebt. People around here are as nasty as anything. Oh, they're 'orrible. I know I'm a little overweight but really that's no reason to torment me. *(with an outraged air)* Why, I was just sitting out on the pier there the other day when two lads sailed up and tried to moor their boat to me. "Oh we're sorry" one said "we didn't know you were real." Oh I can tell you I dashed off in a hurry.

So as I passed these little kids playing, one of them ran to his mother crying, "Mammy, mammy, that fat woman's shadow fell on me and hurt my arm. I think it's broken." Oh it's neck would have been broken if there hadn't been witnesses around . . .

Snooty reenters from left-stage, still drunk.

Snooty: You really should try losing weight, dear lady. Eat your meals in front of a mirror - that way you can only eat half of what's in front of you. Ha, ha, ha.

Fat Lady: *(to Snooty)* Why don't you go and have that mid-life crisis you were talking about.

Snooty: Still can't afford it. Time enough anyway. My Uncle Tom is postponing his until he's sixty.

Fat Lady: Leaving it a bit late, ain't he?

Snooty: No. He says he intends to live to 120 and doesn't want to spoil his chances.

Fat Lady: One hundred and twenty, that's ridiculously old. He'll never make it.

Snooty: Well, since you're well over that age, why shouldn't my Uncle Tom get there one day too.

Fat Lady: *(to SailorBoy)* Well, see what I mean about people around here being vile and disgusting.

DancingGirl: *(curiously)* But I'll bet you've plenty of admirers, haven't you?

Fat Lady: *(smiling and flattered)* Oh yes, no shortage of those.

SailorBoy: *(to DancingGirl)* See, I told you so.

Fat Lady: *(gratefully and pleased to SailorBoy)* Oh thank you. Thank you so much, SailorBoy.

SailorBoy: *(gulps guiltily)* Sure thing. Absolutely.

Fat Lady: You're so nice SailorBoy but most people around here are just horrible.

Skinny: I agree, hen.

SailorBoy: No, no. It's true nobody's perfect but DancingGirl and I wouldn't have come here unless we knew for a fact that the people here were fun.

Skinny: You're very wide of the mark there, cock. Let me tell you, when I was a kid my mum and dad considered me so ugly and skinny they tied me to a pole and set me up in their farm as a scarecrow.

Told me if I did well they'd send me to Scarecrow School to become a professional scaremonger. It was awful.

Dame Knowitall: *(timorously, scared)* And did you scare the crows?

Skinny: Scare them? They were so terrorized they flew back with all the corn they'd stolen for the past three years. But how could anyone do a thing like that to a poor child?

Lotsadebt: Yes, people are not only vile – they've no conscience nowadays. *(he struts around aggressively pointing his index finger at SailorBoy and DancingGirl)* Let me tell you SailorBoy, my home was burgled a while back and about a year later the thief sent back some of the money he stole.

DancingGirl: *(brightly)* That's not all bad.

Lotsadebt: *(agitated and prancing around)* Wait. The thief sent me a note saying - I heard a frightening sermon that pricked my tender conscience. I dashed out of church before the minister had even finished and sent you off this money.

SailorBoy: That sounds reasonable.

Lotsadebt: Really. Then the note ends - If I ever hear the other half of the sermon, I'll send you back the other 90% of the money I stole. *(outragedly)* See, half a sermon gets me only 10% of my money back. What kind of a preacher is that?

Dame Knowitall: Blame the thief not the bible basher.

Lotsadebt: Thief or bible basher, what's the difference? SailorBoy, let me tell you of another case . . .

SailorBoy: *(laughing)* Aw, forget it. I'm sorry I ever mentioned it. Here comes the band. Let's join in.

SailorBoy and DancingGirl look at each other, laugh and shake their heads.

DancingGirl: Well, at least the folks here are fun. We were right about that anyway. And Old Seaside is still the best place in the world to be . . for me.

SailorBoy: Yes and for me too it's the best, just like this old brass band here. There's no modern band that can beat the good old brass. Why, modern brass is crass, an ear-attacking tortured blast. This is the real McCoy coming here.

Enter the Band. *Minimally this should be a Big Drummer, a Fluter, a Trombonist. But others may be added, such as cornet, trumpet, side drums. If extras are not available this scene can be presented by sound only. Actors would then lean over the side of the rock wall and then turn to face the audience as the (offstage) brass band marches along the beach, the actors joining in the song as the music is being played on tape.*

Similarly, there is no need for the bandsmen, even if on stage, to be actually playing the tune. They may mime to the recorded sound of the band. Bandsmen are demonstrative, display their instruments wildly and dance as they march and play. A humorous, satiric, vivid performance is needed as the band and others strut and prance around stage.

DancingGirl: I don't care what they say . . everything here . . the beach, the cafes, the dancing, the people, the fun, the amusements and the brass band - everything in Old Seaside is the best. This is the best of all possible places.

SailorBoy: *(singing and imitating the trombone player)* Here comes the brass band for all the best in boom, boom, boom.

Enter the band *right-stage and play, as the SailorBoy and DancingGirl sing with backing from others:*

BOOM, BOOM, BOOM
Sung: Boisterous and Cheerful

VERSE ONE:

d   r   f - f   d

With a boom, boom, boom

d - r   f - f - f - f   d

We'll liven up and soon

d   r   maw - d - maw - d taw_1 s_1 - s_1 taw_1

We'll be rumbling and bumbling, like the

  d taw_1 - d

Boom of doom

d   r   f   f - s   law

It's the Old Seaside noise

f   maw   d t_1 l_1 s_1

That brings the girls and boys

l_1 t_1 d t_1 l_1 m

To the brass band with all

r   d t_1 l_1 t_1 l_1

The best in boom, boom, boom

l_1 - t_1 d - t_1 l_1 m - r   d t_1 l_1 t_1 l_1

We'll follow the leader with the best in boom

VERSE ONE:

With a boom, boom, boom
We'll liven up and soon
We'll be rumbling and bumbling
Like the boom of doom
It's the Old Seaside noise
That brings the girls and boys
To the brass band with all
The best in boom, boom, boom
We'll follow the leader with the best in boom

VERSE TWO:
When the grand brass band
Goes strutting up the strand
When the trombones go trum
To the sliding of the hand
Then the big brass drum
Goes a rum, a rum, a rum
It's the brass band for all
The best in boom, boom, boom
We'll follow the leader with the best in boom

VERSE THREE:
It's a toot, toot, toot
On the picky little flute
And a vroom, vroom, groan
On the long trombone
And a great drum blatter
That would make the seawaves scatter
It's the brass band with all
The best in boom, boom, boom
We'll follow the leader with the best in boom

Dame Knowitall begins to pass around her empty bucket.

Dame Knowitall: How about a small contribution for the band everybody?

All throw something into the bucket before following the band offstage left. Villain Lotsadebt lurks behind and makes a gimmee, gimmee gesture to the audience.

Lotsadebt: No need for any cash. We'll take an I.O.U. Especially with a few zeros at the end. Listen now – Pay later. I'll get you lot into debt.

Audience: *(in unison)* Oh no you won't.

Lotsadebt: Oh yes I will. Just watch me.

- Curtain -

ACT THREE
THE MAGIC MILE ON THE STRAND

SCENE TWO: DRESS A LITTLE LESS
FOR MORE

The same scene. The tables and chairs of the outdoor cafe are well spread out in this scene to allow for a fairly rapid movement of characters on and off the stage. This is a promenade overlooking the beach which is represented by the same number two backdrop.

Enter Lotsadebt and his pal BillBailiff *dressed as street vendors or hawkers in broad shouldered double breasted suits, wide trousers, wide flashy ties, bright shoes, felt hats, slicked down hair.*
They are hawkers (mobile vendors) selling beachwear and partywear along the promenade to the passing holidaymakers. They carry suitcases full of short dresses, beach shirts, flashy sports shirts with short sleeves, T-shirts, swimwear, etc., all of which they hold up admiringly to the

passersby in a crude and slick effort to get a sale by fast-talking and jesting.

They prance and strut around the stage as they try to make a sale with exaggerated gestures of horror at a refusal or enthusiasm at the possibility of persuading a holidaymaker to buy. They are lively and dynamic at all times.

The passersby tend to be negative towards the efforts of the hawkers, with shaking of heads and hand gestures of refusal and general rejection.

After they have taken up their stations and placed their suitcases open on two of the tables, well back from the flow of passersby, the stream of potential buyers begins.

Enter an Old Fat Woman *carrying a parrot in a cage, a cat in arms and leading a small dog. (real or toys) She is very fat and may be the previous Fat Woman or another similar person. She is well dressed in period costume with gloves, hat, jacket and good shoes.*

Lotsadebt: *(holding up a skimpy pair of beach shorts and later a brief T. shirt)*

Look here hen, how about something more suitable for Old Seaside?

BillBailiff: *(holding up a swimsuit and short skirt)* Yes, something more exciting, lady - like this.

Fat Woman: *(rapidly)* How dare you! Why on earth should I wear that trash?

Lotsadebt: *(swinging his ware in front of Fat Woman)* To make your husband more romantic . . .

Fat Woman: Husband. I never married and don't want one now. What good is a husband?

BillBailiff: *(plaintively)* Keeps you from being lonely?

Fat Woman: Rubbish. I'm never lonely. I have pets. Look, *(holds up cage)* I've a parrot that curses, *(nods to dog)* a dog that drinks beer *(holds up the cat in her arms)* and a cat that passes out in front of the fire. What on earth would I want with a husband?

She cocks her head back defiantly and walks quickly offstage left. As she leaves, the two vendors call after her.

BillBailiff: More success with these. *(holding up a flimsy garment)*

Lotsadebt: You know they say less is more. For more admiring glances and more dates. *(shakes his head in despair, brightens up)* Hey Bill, let's do it in a song and attract a little attention, eh?

BillBailiff: Sure thing.

*They both sing Verse One of **DRESS A LITTLE LESS FOR MORE.***

DRESS A LITTLE LESS FOR MORE
Sung: Fast and Funny

> **VERSE ONE:**
> s   m - m - m   f
> Dress a little less
> r   d t_1 - s_1
> For more success
> l_1 d - d - d   r   d   m
> Dress a little less for more
> m   s   m   f
> More sun, more fun
> r   d - t_1 s_1
> More prizes won
> s_1 l_1 d - d - d - d - d t_1 d
> If you dress a little less for more

VERSE ONE:
Dress a little less
For more success
Dress a little less for more
More sun, more fun
More prizes won
If you dress a little less for more

Enter from rightstage, Dame Knowitall in full turban, dark makeup and eastern robes, carrying her crystal ball and heading, apparently, for her booth (or tent) in a business-like manner. She is intercepted by Villain Lotsadebt and his pal BillBailiff, dancing around and displaying their party apparel.

Lotsadebt: Those robes are too much of a coverup, lass. Get some of this party gear and you'll really draw the crowds.

Dame Knowitall: *(seriously, rapidly and with contempt)* Look, I've got work to go to. How dare you flash that skimpy trash in front of me. I'm a respectable professional woman, you know. Why, that stuff is for women with no brains. I'd have you know that I can foretell fortunes.

BillBailiff: Dress a little less for more success.

Dame Knowitall: Oh yes I get you, more or less, oh yes. You've got it right, there. Why, there's no material in that dress - hardly at all. But you're right. It means more money for you and less dress for the customer. Right. *(she holds crystal ball above her head as though about to break it over Lotsadebt's head)* Right?

Lotsadebt cringes and covers his head with his hands.

BillBailiff: Oh no, you've got us all wrong.   Seaside clothes mean more fun and sun.

Dame Knowitall: *(relenting slightly but still upset)* Well, wear it yourself then. *(replaces the crystal ball under her arm and strides offstage left)*

As she walks off, Lotsadebt and BillBailiff laugh, pat each other on the shoulder and sing Verse 2 of **DRESS.**

> VERSE TWO:
> Dress a little less
> Get more caress
> And glance and dance galore
> Less dress excess
> Means more success
> So dress a little less for more

As they sing this verse, **Enter Millie and Tillie** *heading for the beach and wearing short sleeved, short skirted, low cut beach dresses. Lotsadebt and BillBailiff dance in front of them,* *shaking even flimsier bikinis and short skirts in the air. They sing Verse 3 of* **DRESS** *and dance up and down in unison.*

VERSE THREE:
Dress a little less
For more success
Dress a little less for more
More lass, more class
More lads with brass
Dress a little less for more

Millie: *(outraged)* Even less than what I'm wearing in public. What do you take me for? Besides, I've got all those silly things you're selling, for private wear, of course. *(she sniffs in a prudish gesture)* All I need to wear is a watch. Why haven't you got any watches?

Lotsadebt and BillBailiff look blank.

Lotsadebt: *(gulping and recovering somewhat but still confused at the onslaught)* Oh yes, of course, err . . a watch is all you need. Oh no, you've got to wear more than a watch if you wish to retain respectability.

Millie: *(interrupting and hitting him over the head with her parasol)* You're a real wit - a nitwit. Take that.

Millie strides offstage left, outraged and still aggressive. Tillie, who has been watching, hands on hips, angrily steps out to follow her but turns and begins to berate the two vendors.

Tillie: Yes. I've got all those kinds of gear too but what I really need is a pair of sunglasses. Why aren't you selling cheap glasses?

Lotsadebt: But lady, why would you need glasses?

Tillie: *(aggressively, shrilly, trembling, poking her parasol at him)* Why would I need glasses? To see who's asking me for a date, of course. Why else?

BillBailiff: Aw don't be hard on a bloke, judging him by his appearance. Never judge a book by its cover you know.

Tillie: *(infuriated, shrilly)* So I'm a pickup, am I . . a tramp? So I should date anyone, no matter what he looks like, eh? So you're telling me I can't use my judgment about fellahs, eh? So you think I should grab anything that's going, anything in trousers, any man I can get, without even looking him over, eh? Oh really, what do I need with glasses, huh? Take that.

She hits BillBailiff across the rear with her parasol and strides offstage left, turning around as she leaves to stick her nose in the air, disgustedly.

Lotsadebt and BillBailiff spread their hands helplessly and shrug at each other.

Enter from right-stage, Snooty, *white boater, blazer and slacks, red waistcoat and blue tie, staggering elegantly and leaning on a walking stick. He nods patronizingly as he intends to pass by the two vendors.*

Lotsadebt and BillBailiff recover their disappointment, nod at each other significantly and point towards Snooty.

BillBailiff: *(winks at Lotsadebt)* This one looks like a good mark, a true potential customer.

Lotsadebt: Here, Snooty, here's some real party and beachwear for you. You're wearing too many clothes. *(he holds up his wares)*

Snooty: Am I? Good heavens, you're not suggesting that I should wear those practically non-existent shorts and spotted shirts, are you?

Lotsadebt: Sure, cock and why not? Listen, squire, these party shirts and shorts is just the thing to make you popular with the ladies. Help you get a date mate! See?

Snooty: *(looking at shorts and shirts in disgust)* I'm sorry . . . I'm already married.

Lotsadebt: So this is a good way to scare off the old wife and brighten you up to marry some nice rich old widder, eh? How's about that?

Snooty: One should never marry a widow. She might be making a habit of it.

BillBailiff: Well then guv, how's about livening up things between you and the wife like, since you're such a good family man.

Snooty: *(rolling his eyes a little)* My wife and I are mature and sensible and not interested in such frivolities. Of course, I don't mind a little flirtation now and again.

Lotsadebt: That's it. *(teasingly)* Just for a flirtation try some of these, guv. Experts all tell us that an older man like you should be able to get romantic at least once or twice a year.

Snooty: *(counting shortsightedly on his fingers)* How many times?

Lotsadebt: *(holding up two fingers)* Once or twice a year, mate.

Snooty: *(surprised)* Really? Well, don't tell my wife, it might make her jealous.

Lotsadebt and BillBailiff sing Verse Four of DRESS and dance up and down in unison.

VERSE FOUR:
Dress a little less
For more success
Dress a little less for more
More flash, more bash
More Seaside brash
Dress a little less for more

Snooty: How much?

Lotsadebt: *(holding up shorts)* Four half crowns, tell yer what, two dollars.

Snooty is confused and scratches his head.

BillBailiff: *(holding up spotted tee-shirt)* It used to be half a quid but you can have it for 10 bob.

Snooty is still confused and sticks his finger in his ear and shakes his head.

Lotsadebt: Here, I'll bring it down from two dollars to 10 shillings. *(slaps his knee)* Tell you what - 20 tanners takes it. Right, cock. How about that for a sale, eh, squire?

Snooty tries counting on his fingers but gives up.

Snooty: Why you two dolts couldn't tell the difference between a tanner, a sixpence and two thrupenny bits. You're just two moneygrabbers. That stuff is just cheap junk. You know most people are silly with money.

BillBailiff: Look here mate, it's the same thing when you buy anybody a present and they buy you one back.

Lotsadebt: Yes, I agree with Bill.

Snooty: But there's something I don't understand.
The two hawkers listen and nod blankly.
I take my wife out for our anniversary. Buy her a nice dinner at Rovano's. So she eats it. *(slurring)* So I eat it. See?
They nod.
So what do we end up with? Nothing for her, nothing for me - all eaten O.K?

They nod blankly.
So . . *(he marshals himself manfully and straightens up)* So what does Rovano end up with? Eh? Forty quid - right?
The others nod, stunned.
 Now, I ask you, whose anniversary is it anyway - mine and my old lady's - or Rovano's?
The others shake their heads blankly.
Same thing for birthdays *(hic)* I buy her a present and she buys me a present. So we both get something we don't really want or we would have bought it ourselves. See?
The others nod fascinated.
But the giftstore lady, Old Lily, she gets something she does really want - about forty quid. Get it? So whose birthday is it supposed to be? Tell me that?
The others shrug, shake their heads
and spread their hands at a loss.
Doesn't make sense to me. So I'll have to say 'no' to all those junky, near invisible clothes. I'd rather just keep the money for something sensible like a nice tall drink. Sorry old chaps and all that.

Lotsadebt: *(snapping out of his daze)* Aw, come on guvner. Have a heart. See, just 10 bob.

Snooty: Yes or four half crowns. I heard you.

Lotsadebt and BillBailiff join together in pleadingly singing all of **DRESS** *as Snooty staggers offstage left, still making vaguely negative gestures, shaking his head, holding up his hand in a 'no thanks' wave of farewell. Raises his hat to audience as he leaves.*

Snooty leaves left and DancingGirl and the SailorBoy enter right. *At least half of the song should be addressed to them. They dance center and join in the song and this time sing straight through without interruption.*

DRESS A LITTLE LESS FOR MORE

VERSE ONE:
Dress a little less
For more success
Dress a little less for more
More sun, more fun
More prizes won
If you dress a little less for more

VERSE TWO:
Dress a little less
Get more caress
And glance and dance galore
Less dress excess
Means more success
So dress a little less for more

VERSE THREE:
Dress a little less
For more success
Dress a little less for more
More lass, more class
More lads with brass
Dress a little less for more

VERSE FOUR:
Dress a little less
For more success
Dress a little less for more
More flash, more bash
More Seaside brash
Dress a little less for more

VERSE FIVE:
Dress a little less
Get more caress
And glance and dance galore
Less dress excess
Means more success
If you dress a little less for more

As the song ends, Lotsadebt and his pal BillBailiff pack up their suitcases, philosophically shake their heads and prepare to leave for brighter prospects elsewhere.

Lotsadebt: All right, Bill, we're not doing ourselves any good here. Let's move on to a more high-class clientele.

BillBailiff: Right, you old rapscallion. Let's skedaddle and try somewhere else.

Maybe catch the ones with brass going into the market, eh?

They leave stage right.

DancingGirl and SailorBoy catch their breath and pause after singing and dancing.

DancingGirl: Well, wasn't that a bit of Old Seaside, for sure?

SailorBoy: *(nostalgically)*
That's what Old Seaside was all about
Those two spivs, so ill-matched to each other physically
One short and one big
And yet getting along so well
That was the spirit of Old Seaside
And their song and their silly party rags
That was the bright and bouncy
The same old brashy and trashy
The same old, dowdy and rowdy
Old Seaside
That's what made it such fun
It wasn't just the sand
And the sun.
If it had been quiet and grand

Or wishy-washy or even bland
No one ever would have saved
All year, just to hear the band
In a place where no one ever misbehaved
This was the trusted and the true
The tested and tried
The same old fun that you
Always knew
Was always new
In Old Seaside

DancingGirl:
Then I've proven my promise
I said I would show that Old Seaside
hidden away
Has never really died
Rather it lives and thrives
Along the Magic Mile
There lives the tear, the smile
Where we all laughed and cried
Where we all passed the best
Part of our early lives
Way down at the seaside in the place called
Old Seaside

I've shown you the places where the good
old days still live and so I'll leave you here

a while to walk and talk with the good old friends along the Magic Mile. Among the same funny, silly, wonderful people who have always been there and always will.

DancingGirl leaves stage left.

SailorBoy: But wait . . *(calling out)* come back . . ahh . . she's gone *(looks onto the far distance offstage left)* . . lost in the bumble and bustle, disappeared among the many in Old Seaside. *(sighing)* Ah, was she real or was she just a vision?

*The music of **GOOD OLD DAYS** is heard, somewhat slowly and sadly. The lights dim slightly as SailorBoy dances as one alone and sad, stretching out his hands to the encroaching shadows as the lights fade.*

- Curtain -

ACT FOUR
DANCINGGIRL FROM THE GOOD OLD DAYS

SCENE ONE: THE OLD POSTCARD

*A few weeks later back in today's Old Seaside at the **GOOD OLD DAYS CAFE** with outdoor garden and street seats, in front-stage. (same scene as in Act One, Scene One) It is a calm and beautiful evening. A large postcard is in the background.*

***Enter from right-stage SailorBoy,** looks around nostalgically and walks about and looks at a postcard in his hand from time to time.*

SailorBoy: It was right here that DancingGirl first appeared to me, just as I sang a song about the good old days.

sings verse of GOOD OLD DAYS.

VERSE TWO:

　s　　fe　　s - l　　　s - m　　　d　　m m - m - r　　*m* m
Back in those days they were relaxed and cheerful people
　s　　fe　s - l - s m d　　r r　　　r　d　　*r*
Folks got to talking in a friendly sort of way
　r　　m - m　　f - m　　　m - m　　　l₁
There was a casual kind of person then
　l₁　m　m - m　　m　　m *r*
That you rarely meet today
　s　s - l - s　　m　　d　　m　　m - m
But if I could just walk down a street
　m　　m　m - r　　f - m　　*l₁*
Where the oldtime music plays
　l₁　d　　r　r r　　d　r - d　m f　　m
That good old music is enough to take me
　m - m　d - m　　m　*d*
Back to the good old days

I wonder if she's just a memory come alive? She left suddenly and disappeared into thin air. She seemed like beauty from the past returned on life's strange waters. Yet, she's not a person from my past but more like a memory of many cheerful girls and yet, she seemed real enough when she was here earlier. Yes *(he nods to himself and looks at postcard)* she was alive all right and a most beautiful dancer.

Well, let me see . . . *(he rubs his chin and thinks)* When I sang a song about the good old days, she suddenly appeared. Good old music that I haven't heard for a long time seemed to come alive out of the past as though it came out of an old phonograph lying hidden away in the attic of lost memories.

*He looks at the postcard and reflects. Sings **WISH YOU WERE HERE, AGAIN.***

REFRAIN:

| d | d | t_1 | d | r | d - l_1 | l_1 |

Yes, there's the white bright shining lights

| d | r | d | r | m | d |

And here's my keepsake pen

| f | f | m | f | f | s - f | m |

And now it writes Old Seaside nights

| d | d | d | m | f | *f* |

Wish you were here, again

| d | d | d | m | f | *f* |

Wish you were here, again

I do believe that there's magic in this place tonight.

As the SailorBoy speaks, the lights fade slightly and spotlight focuses on the figure of DancingGirl in the large postcard that forms the backdrop. SailorBoy addresses, at times, the form of DancingGirl in the card. As he looks at her the lights dim and spotlight focuses on the postcard in the SailorBoy's hand.

__Enter DancingGirl.__ SailorBoy is first surprised then overjoyed to see her as he leaps in the air. She dances around him in a circle. Then, as they talk, they dance slowly to the music of __GOOD OLD DAYS.__ She breaks away and dances on her own, right-stage then dances back.

DancingGirl: So, what of the good old days? What did you think, is today just as good as the good old days?

SailorBoy: *(wags his head from side to side, flicks his right thumb to the left and the right)* Well, yes and no. The music and the movies were definitely better.

DancingGirl: *(with empathy)* Maybe so but life was a struggle for many back then.

SailorBoy: So tell me, are you real or just a ghost or a memory come alive? Why do you come and go so mysteriously?

DancingGirl: Well . . now that you mention it *(looks at her watch)* it's almost time for me to go.

SailorBoy: *(pleading)* Stay a while and dance.

Sailorboy sings as they dance briefly to musical backing from the melody of

SEE YOU AROUND
Sung: Slow and Sentimental

s_1 m - m   r   m - m   d   m f m   r
It's strange how the rivers of memory flow
s_1 r - r   d r - r   d   m - m   r s_1
You seem to remind me of someone I know
s_1 m - m   m - m   f   m l_1 m maw - r
Someone I remember from long, long ago
r s_1 - d m   m   m - d
So, I'll see you around

- Curtain -

ACT FOUR
THE DANCINGGIRL OF GOOD OLD DAYS

SCENE TWO: SEE YOU AROUND

*The scene is the same. Curtain rises on SailorBoy and DancingGirl, front center. The music of **SEE YOU AROUND** is still playing. This is to achieve continuity between this scene and the previous one as reflected in part by the music. It then fades away as SailorBoy and DancingGirl dance. The SailorBoy sings a verse of*

SEE YOU AROUND
Sung: Slow and Sentimental

> s_1 m - m   r   m - m d m   f   m   *r*
> I sometimes stop into a place that I know
> s_1 r   r - d   r   r   d   m - m   r s_1
> Where the music is very relaxing and low
> s_1 m - m   m - m   f   m l_1 m   maw $- r$
> It might be a nice place that you'd like to go
>   r s_1 - d   m   m   m $- d$
> So, I'll see you around

SailorBoy and DancingGirl again take up center-stage as the mood changes from gaiety gradually back to one of romance and nostalgia. The lighting focuses mainly on SailorBoy and the DancingGirl.

*The music of **SEE YOU AROUND** is played by way of background as SailorBoy and DancingGirl dance slowly together throughout the following dialogue. There can be slight vocal backing from a chorus offstage.*

DancingGirl: Well, surely now it is really time for me to go.

SailorBoy: Will you come back?

DancingGirl: Maybe.

SailorBoy: But not certainly.

DancingGirl: *(smiling)* Not certainly but most certainly sometime. As the song says "When oldtime music sings and swings and oldtime songs are sadly sung. I'll come, as a DancingGirl, to weave the scenes of love long gone."

SailorBoy: You will return to where the oldtime music plays?

DancingGirl: Yes, wherever the good oldtime music is playing, I'll see you around. Wherever I hear that good old music - for instance . . the music of the ***GOOD OLD DAYS.***

*Enter Snooty, the Drunk and the Fat Lady. They sing part of **DRINK YOUR TEA** and **FISH AND CHIPS.***

DRINK YOUR TEA
Sung: Jolly

VERSE ONE:

d   d   d   d l_1 - d
Don't get scared or skittish
f   f f r - f
Fight to the finish
d   d   d d r - d
Be proud to be British
d l_1 s_1
Drink your tea
d   d   d   d l_1 - d
No matter how you suffer
f f f   f r - f
Keep a true stiff upper
f f f   f m - m
Eat a good fish supper
f   s   f
Drink your tea

THE FISH AND CHIPS SONG
Sung: Fast

VERSE ONE AND REFRAIN:

s   d - d   m   s   d^1 t
O I'll have some fish and chips please
d^1 r^1 l - l - l - l
If that's all right with you
 f   r - r - r   f   t - t - t
Not too much grease - some mushy peas
 l   s   s   s - f   m
And salt and vinegar too
 s   d - d   m - s d^1 - d^1 t
No more the dainty dinner do
  d^1 r^1 l - l - l - l
No more them dunking dips
 l   s   s - s   s - t   t   l
I say if it's all right with you
  s - s   s   f   r   d
I'll have some fish and chips

DancingGirl: Or when I hear the song of the sideshows.

Enter the sideshow sillies, Millie and Tillie and sing part of SEASIDE BY THE SEA.

SEE YOU AROUND

Sung: Jolly

VERSE ONE:
   d   d   f   s   l - s - f
Y'all come down to Seaside Town
   f - s   f   r   d
Seaside by the Sea
   d   l₁   d   f   l - l   s   f
Along the strand and over the sand
   f s   f   m   f   s
Is all the fun you need
   d   l₁ - d r - *f* f s   l - l   s   *f*
Some love to go to the slopes of snow
   f - f - s - f   r   d
Seems kind of cold to me
   r - d - r - m - *f*   s   l   s   *f*
But boats are afloat with friendly folk
   f - s - r   m   d   *f*
In Seaside by the Sea

SailorBoy: And when the Brass Band treks along the sands, then you will hear and come again.

DancingGirl: Yes.

Enter the Brass Band and all sing part of BOOM, BOOM, BOOM.

SEE YOU AROUND

Sung: Boisterous and Cheerful

VERSE ONE:

  d   r   f - f   d
With a boom, boom, boom
d - r f - f - f - f   d
We'll liven up and soon
  d   r maw - d - maw - d taw$_1$ s$_1$ - s$_1$ taw$_1$
We'll be rumbling and bumbling, like the
  d taw$_1$ - d
Boom of doom
  d   r   f   f - s   law
It's the Old Seaside noise
  f   maw   d   t$_1$ l$_1$ s$_1$
That brings the girls and boys
 l$_1$ t$_1$ d   t$_1$ l$_1$ m
To the brass band with all
  r   d   t$_1$ l$_1$ t$_1$ l$_1$
The best in boom, boom, boom
 l$_1$ - t$_1$ d - t$_1$ l$_1$ m - r d t$_1$ l$_1$ t$_1$ l$_1$
We'll follow the leader with the best in boom

DancingGirl: And I do love to shop and get a bargain, so the oldtime street vendors are my favorite. When I hear their song, I'll come and join in the fun. *Enter the two street Vendors (Villain Lotsadebt and his pal BillBailiff) and sing part of DRESS A LITTLE LESS FOR MORE.*

Sung: Fast and Funny

VERSE ONE:
s m - m - m f
Dress a little less
r   d t_1 - s_1
For more success
l_1 d - d - d r d   m
Dress a little less for more
m   s   m   f
More sun, more fun
r   d - t_1 s_1
More prizes won
s_1 l_1 d - d - d - d - d t_1 d
If you dress a little less for more

*SailorBoy and DancingGirl take center-stage again and the others range around in a circle. SailorBoy takes her hand and they sing, **SEE YOU AROUND**. Each singing alternate verses.*

SEE YOU AROUND
Sung: Slow and Sentimental

VERSE ONE:

s₁   m - m   r   m - m d m f m   r

It's strange how the rivers of memory flow

s₁   r - r   d r - r   d   m - m r s₁

You seem to remind me of someone I know

s₁ m - m   m - m f   m   l₁ m maw - r

Someone I remember from long, long ago

r s₁ - d m m   m - d

So, I'll see you around

SailorBoy:
It's strange how the rivers of memory flow
You seem to remind me of someone I know
Someone I remember from long, long ago
So, I'll see you around

DancingGirl:
I don't fall in love the way some people do
Head over heels and feeling all blue
But I do have a feeling I'd like to know you
So, I'll see you around

SailorBoy:
I sometimes stop into a place that I know
Where the music is very relaxing and low
It might be a nice place that you'd like to go
So, I'll see you around

DancingGirl:

There are strangers who meet in and out on the tide
There are some that the wild winds separate far and wide
There are also a few who will drift side by side
So, I'll see you around

*The dance ends. They stand together center-stage. The other singers and dancers are now silent and range around in the background as SailorBoy sings Verse One **THE GOOD OLD DAYS** and holds DancingGirl in his arms.*

VERSE ONE:

```
   s    fe    s - l     s - m - d      m  m - m     r     m  m
```
One of these days I'm going back to see Old Seaside
```
   s    fe    s - l     s - m - d      r  r - r     d     r
```
One of these days I'm gonna take it nice and slow
```
   r    m - m    f - m    m - m    l₁
```
And just go drifting in and out
```
 l₁   m - m    m    m    m - m    r
```
The places that I used to go
```
 s   s - l - s    m    d    m    m - m
```
I may never find the same old crowd
```
   m    m    m - r    f - m    l₁
```
Where the oldtime music plays
```
 l₁   d    r    r    r - d - r - d    m    s    f    m
```
But I'd like to listen to the songs we sang then
```
   m - m    d - m    m    d
```
Back in the good old days

SailorBoy takes DancingGirl's hand. She kneels and bows to the audience, then dances away to backstage and disappears into the old postcard to join the others.

SailorBoy: *(sadly)* So all I've left is a postcard from dear Old Seaside. That's all you get from the seaside, a postcard to send to a friend or a postcard from a friend you met there. A postcard to lie in the old attic of your past life but you also get something you cannot see but only feel, the best memories anyone ever had. Memories of fun and beaches and new friends and romance and lazy days in the sun and, really, aren't memories the only things that never wear out, that seem to get better as the years go by. Surely memories are the only thing in the world that we can keep with us forever.

So DancingGirl, wherever you are, I will put these old time songs into a stage show so that the oldtime music will be sung and you will appear to me time and again out of the magic postcard.

(to audience) So whenever you hear that song ***THE GOOD OLD DAYS*** - look for DancingGirl singing and dancing to bring alive a memory of the past.

SailorBoy joins DancingGirl in the backdrop procession, in front of the giant postcard, becoming a part of the backdrop. The lights dim and the other characters, including DancingGirl, also take their places in front of the backdrop along with the Sergeant Major and drum, the Piper and pipes, the Fluter and flute and the others.

Lights slowly brighten until the audience can see all the characters in line in the now "living postcard" with white borders and the caption greeting BEST WISHES FROM OLD SEASIDE. *The characters and the caption are all highlighted in turn.*

Then . . . Lights fade.

- **Curtain** –

Suddenly Villain Lotsadebt emerges in front of the curtain from the left-stage. He points around the audience.

LotsaDebt: So I didn't get much of their money but just you wait and see what I'm going to do next. Me and my pal BillBailiff are coming round to your house to get your money. You'd be surprised what stupid schemes we can talk you in to.

Audience: Oh no you won't.

Lotsadebt: Oh yes I will.
Suddenly BillBailiff joins his pal.

BillBailiff: And if you can't pay up, I'm more than reasonable. I'm willing to take your car instead or that big flat screen TV or even better that holiday in the sun next year.

Audience: Oh no you won't.

BillBailiff: Oh yes I will.

They sing part of Dress a Little Less to the audience.

VERSE ONE:
  s m - m - m f
Dress a little less
  r   d t_1 - s_1
For more success
  l_1 d - d - d r   d   m
Dress a little less for more
  m   s   m   f
More sun, more fun
  r   d - t_1 s_1
More prizes won
s_1 l_1 d - d - d - d - d t_1 d
If you dress a little less for more

They stick out their tongues, put their thumbs in their ears and wiggle their fingers at the audience.

As they leave left-stage sneering and shaking their fists they shout at the audience again.

Lotsadebt and BillBailiff: We're going to get your money, just wait and see.

Audience: Oh no you won't.

Lotsadebt and BillBailiff: Oh yes, we will.

Audience: Oh no you won't.

Dame Knowitall comes on stage from the right carrying a large broom that she shakes at the two villains.

Dame Knowitall: Don't worry everyone, I'll make sure these two moneygrabbers don't get any of your money or your holiday in the sun.

She sweeps the pair off the stage to the cheers of the audience.

Audience: Hooray for Dame Knowitall.

- Final Curtain –

END OF PLAYSCRIPT

APPENDIX
FIVE FINGER EXERCISE
Simple Instructions on How to Play the Tunes

Music is presented in the form of tonic sol-fa. Tonic sol-fa is the written form of music for both beginners and virtuosos – those who do not need guidance on timing, arrangements or chords – those who need only the basic tune.

1. Hitting the Right Note
2. White Keys - Stick-On Labels
3. Black Keys - Stick-On Labels
4. Getting the Timing Right
5. Summary

HITTING THE RIGHT NOTE

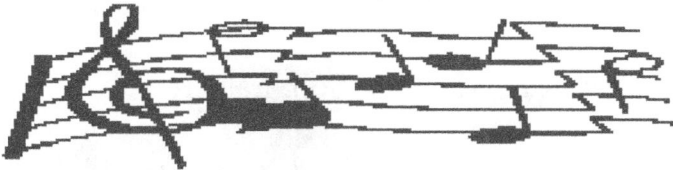

C is the white note just to the left of the two black notes side by side. Find Middle C on your keyboard. A register is the level of a set of tonic sol-fa. Here is the location of Middle C on a standard three register keyboard. The white note in the exact middle of any keyboard is Middle C (in staff) and Doh (in tonic sol-fa).

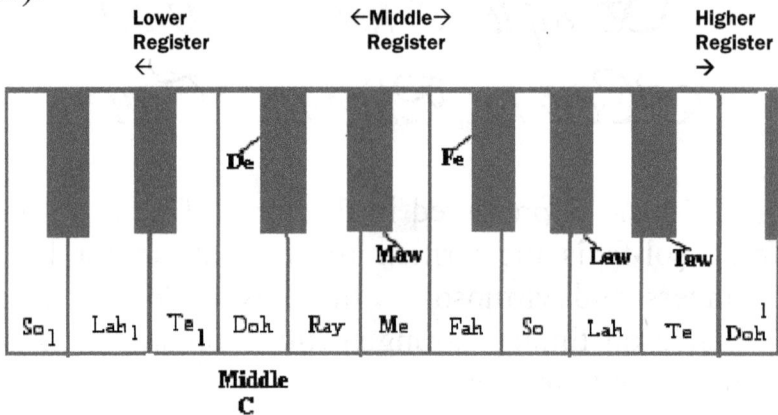

| Lower Register ← | ←Middle→ Register | Higher Register → |

De   Fe

Maw   Law   Taw

So_1 | Lah_1 | Te_1 | Doh | Ray | Me | Fah | So | Lah | Te | Doh^1

Middle C

The tunes in this songbook can all be played on these three middle registers. Larger keyboards may have additional higher or lower registers but these will not be needed for the simple basic tunes in this book.

C is always Doh and going up from Middle C is the central set of tonic sol-fa:

Doh, Ray, Me, Fah, Soh, Lah, Te.

The next note is also a C and is the Doh higher than Central Doh. This starts off the next register of tonic sol-fa notes.

The Middle Set of tonic sol-fa have no subscript or superscript: d, r, m, f, s, l, t.

The Lower Register (set of tonic sol-fa) have subscripts as follows: $d_1, r_1, m_1, f_1, s_1, l_1, t_1$.

The Higher Register (set of tonic sol-fa) have superscripts as follows: $d^1, r^1, m^1, f^1, s^1, l^1, t^1$.

Here is a complete set of labels, for the white and black keys, to stick onto your central basic keyboard.

WHITE KEYS: STICK-ON LABELS FOR YOUR KEYBOARD

LOWER REGISTER	Doh_1	Ray_1	Me_1	Fah_1	Soh_1	Lah_1	Te_1
MIDDLE REGISTER	Doh	Ray	Me	Fah	Soh	Lah	Te
HIGHER REGISTER	Doh^1	Ray^1	Me^1	Fah^1	Soh^1	Lah^1	Te^1

WHITE STICK-ON NOTE INSTRUCTIONS

These are to be stuck on to your keyboard to show you which notes to play as you follow the Tonic Sol-fa music set out in each song.

1. The seven white notes with subscripts (lower register) lead up to Middle C.

2. Middle C starts off the middle register of seven white notes that have neither subscripts nor superscript.

3. The seven white notes with superscripts (higher register) follows on after the middle register.

Only the last three white notes of the lower register and the first white note of the higher register are shown with the middle register in the keyboard diagram.

THE BLACK KEYS

The black keys in each register are as follows: de, maw, fe, law, taw.

The five black keys in the lower register have subscripts
The five black keys in the middle register have no subscripts or superscripts
The five black keys in the higher register have superscripts.

Here are the three sets of labels to stick onto the black notes on your keyboard.

LOWER REGISTER	De_1	Maw_1	Fe_1	Law_1	Taw_1
MIDDLE REGISTER	De	Maw	Fe	Law	Taw
HIGHER REGISTER	De^1	Maw^1	Fe^1	Law^1	Taw^1

GETTING THE TIMING RIGHT

(1) Notes that are grouped together have hyphens between them - to show that they are played together. (eg: d - f - l). This does not mean that such notes are speeded up, only that they are joined together.

(2) Notes that are to be held longer than average are written in italics - that is to say they are sloped to the right (eg: *d* or *s*).

(3) Try to follow the hints at the head of each tune (eg: slow and simple or fast and warlike).Keep a steady and regular beat whether the tune is fast or slow (eg: tap your foot or get a friend to tap out an even measured beat).

SUMMARY

Below is a diagram of all three registers - Lower, Middle and Higher. Of course, on many keyboards and pianos there are more than these three registers but these keys are all that you will need to play the simple tunes in this songbook

Lower Register **Middle Register** **Higher Register**

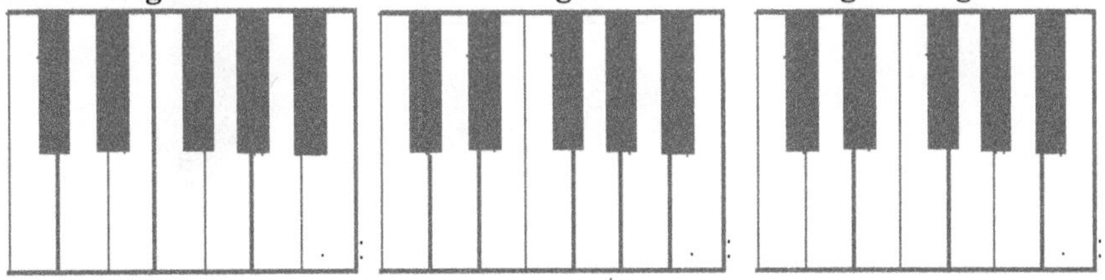

← Middle C →

← Subscripts → **← Superscripts →**

BRIEF INSTRUCTIONS

1. Cut out the squares and stick them on to the black and white keys.

2. Hit the notes asked for in the tonic sol-fa tunes, trying to hear each melody as a whole and keeping a steady beat.

> **Key to
> Tonic Sol-fa
> Notes**
> D = doh
> R = ray
> M = me
> F = fah
> S = soh
> L = lah
> T = te

WHITE KEYS: STICK-ON LABELS
FOR YOUR KEYBOARD

LOWER REGISTER	Doh$_1$	Ray$_1$	Me$_1$	Fah$_1$	Soh$_1$	Lah$_1$	Te$_1$
MIDDLE REGISTER	Doh	Ray	Me	Fah	Soh	Lah	Te
HIGHER REGISTER	Doh^1	Ray^1	Me^1	Fah^1	Soh^1	Lah^1	Te^1

BLACK KEYS: STICK-ON LABELS
FOR YOUR KEYBOARD

LOWER REGISTER	De$_1$	Maw$_1$	Fe$_1$	Law$_1$	Taw$_1$
MIDDLE REGISTER	De	Maw	Fe	Law	Taw
HIGHER REGISTER	De^1	Maw^1	Fe^1	Law^1	Taw^1

HOW TO IMPROVE YOUR SINGING

In singing these songs there are seven main aspects of singing to check out and practice towards perfection. (There are also several more subtle, complex and minor aspects which only a real-life music teacher could explain. Each aspect of singing calls for separate exercises as well as putting all six together.

1. Voice Quality
Largely a given, quality can be developed by practice, healthy diet and deep breathing.

2. Diction
Concentrate on sharp clear pronunciation to achieve understanding on the part of the listener. Aim for sounds that most people with standard English, not accents, will understand.

3. Projection
Throw out the voice until all the audience can hear it. Every word must always reach the listener.

4. Phrasing
A phrase is a group of words and notes that are grouped together. Watch how the sounds and words hang together and change the combinations until it sounds right to you in your opinion. What is right for one singer may not be right for another.

5. Feeling
Try to imagine how the sender of the message would feel and think. Develop a dramatic empathy, a oneness with the message of the song so that it comes over as genuine.

6. Rhythm
Keep an even beat or a creative subtly uneven one. Tap your foot on the ground or follow a drummer, or hand claps (see also the section on timing).

7. True Notes
Make sure that the note you play is the right one. Listen to a self-tape and compare your notes with those sung by a friend or played on a keyboard or other instrument. Sometimes it helps to close your eyes and listen well.

8. Find a Teacher
If you can, find a good singing teacher with top credentials or at least get a musical friend to critique you.

THE END

www.ingramcontent.com/pod-product-compliance
Lightning Source LLC
Chambersburg PA
CBHW061727020426
42331CB00006B/1139